Home for the Holidays

FESTIVE RECIPES FOR CELEBRATING THE MOST WONDERFUL TIME OF YEAR!

ASHLEY MANILA

BAKER BY NATURE

For my mom.

I miss you so much, but especially during the holidays.

Contents

Introduction | 1

PART ONE: HOLIDAY MENUS

Holiday Party Menus | 6

PART TWO: THE RECIPES

1 / BREAKFAST & BRUNCH

Brown Butter–Orange Ricotta Pancakes | 16

Fluffy Cinnamon Rolls | 19

Bacon & Caramelized Onion Quiche | 23

Nutella® Beignets | 25

Sausage & Potato Breakfast Casserole | 28

Sugar & Spice Donuts | 31

Cranberry Orange Scones | 32

Cinnamon Apple French Toast | 35

Double Chocolate–Banana Bundt Cake | 36

Morning Glory Muffins | 39

2 / APPETIZERS & SNACKS

Whipped Ricotta Toast with Olives & Almonds | 42

Lemon-Rosemary Chicken Wings | 45

Ultimate Meatball Sliders | 47

Caramelized Onion Dip Snack Board | 51

Garlic Parmesan Popcorn | 55

Prosciutto-Wrapped Jalapeño Poppers | 56

Italian Hoagie Party Platter | 59

Brie Bites with Cranberry Chutney | 60

Mini Crab Cakes with Spicy Remoulade Sauce | 65

Four-Cheese Spinach Dip | 66

3 / MEALS

Holiday Hens with Wild Rice Pilaf | 70

Garlicky Shrimp Polenta | 73

Pan-Seared Cod in Lemon-Caper Sauce | 74

Meatball & Spinach Baked Ziti | 77

Lemon Risotto with Brown Butter Scallops | 79

Special Occasion Roast Beef with Roasted Carrots | 83

Chicken Parmesan for a Crowd | 84

Rigatoni Bolognese with Garlic Bread | 87

Herb-Crusted Salmon with Mashed Potatoes | 90

4 / SIDES

Rosemary & Garlic Roasted Potatoes | 94

Italian Wedding Soup | 97

Parker House Rolls | 98

Feel-Good Holiday Salad | 103

Pasta Fagioli | 104

Creamy White Cheddar Macaroni & Cheese | 107

Balsamic Brussels Sprouts with Pancetta & Pomegranate Seeds | 108

Crowd-Pleasing Caesar Salad with Garlic Bread Croutons | 111

Warm Bacon & Green Bean Salad | 115

5 / DESSERTS

Eggnog Tiramisu | 118

New York–Style Cheesecake with Grand Marnier® Cranberry Sauce | 121

Extra-Creamy Cannoli | 125

Chocolate Peppermint Cake | 126

Pumpkin Cheesecake with Pecan Praline Sauce | 129

Christmas Funfetti Sheet Cake | 133

Black Forest Cheesecake | 137

Sparkling Champagne Cupcakes | 141

Cranberry Cherry Pie | 145

Gingerbread Celebration Cake | 149

6 / COOKIES & BARS

My Favorite Butter Cookies | 154

Triple Chocolate Brownies | 159

Oatmeal Chocolate Chunk Cookies | 160

Cranberry-Pistachio Biscotti | 163

Lemon White Chocolate Macadamia Nut Cookies | 167

Chocolate Crinkles | 168

Molasses Cream Pies | 171

Salted Caramel Apple Pie Bars | 173

Peanut Butter M&M® Cookies | 176

Brown Butter Blondies | 179

7 / CANDY

Cherry-Almond Chocolate Bark | 182

Bourbon Butter Pecan Fudge | 185

Chocolate-Covered Peanut Butter Christmas Trees | 186

Kahlúa Peppermint Mocha Chocolate Truffles | 190

Dark Chocolate & Sea Salt Caramels | 193

Chocolate-Covered Almond Toffee | 197

Coconut-Pecan Truffles | 198

Peppermint Bark | 201

8 / COCKTAILS & BEVERAGES

European-Style Hot Chocolate with Peppermint Marshmallows | 204

Holiday Sangria | 208

Thick & Creamy Eggnog | 211

Pomegranate Party Punch | 212

Rosemary Lemonade | 215

Cranberry-Ginger Moscow Mules | 216

Cozy Mulled Cider | 219

Brunch Bloody Mary Bar | 220

Piña Colada Sunrise Mimosas | 223

PART THREE: ENTERTAINING 101

Baking Secrets | 227

Ashley's Entertaining Tips | 229

Crafting a Guest List | 233

Acknowledgments | 237

Index | 240

Introduction

What do you love most about the holidays?

This is a question I pondered endlessly throughout the conception of this book! And one I frequently returned to as I was compiling the recipes, menus, and ideas you'll find in these pages.

The answer I arrived at over and over again? *Home*. The comfort of home . . . home-cooked meals . . . inviting people into your home . . . and cozy days spent at home baking for friends and neighbors. It's truly the perfect season to fully embrace being a homebody! From popping cookies in the oven, to hosting a holiday movie night, to inviting a few friends over for a family-style feast or a round of festive cocktails, it's just so easy to get swept up in the holiday spirit!

My holiday spirit was cultivated at a young age. I grew up in a house where Christmas was a really, *really* big deal! My mom was an expert at taking the little we had and making it absolute magic! Her ideas were crafty (some might even say scrappy), creative, and totally unconventional. She wrapped all of our doors in shiny wrapping paper and tied them with giant bows so they looked like presents. She'd let us sneak nibbles of cookie dough and she would dance with us on beds and tables as Christmas music played (just a little too loudly) in the background. On Christmas Eve, we drank copious amounts of eggnog, baked cookies for Santa, and always ended up opening *at least* one present before finally being cajoled into bed by the promise of more fun to come in the morning. It was these simple but oh-so-special childhood experiences that started me on my lifelong love affair with the holidays.

Over the years, the biggest evolution in our holiday celebrations was the food. Growing up, a lot of the food mentioned in my memories was store-bought. But as my passion for cooking and baking grew, I quickly—and happily—assumed the role of holiday party planner and chef! It was only a matter of time before homemade cookies, cinnamon rolls, and ultra-thick hot cocoa became a part of our highly anticipated yearly traditions.

Up until the year my mom passed, we would spend *hours* on the phone discussing menus, plans, and presents. But we mainly obsessed over the menu. Always adding on last-minute extras and fretting over whether there'd be enough food for everyone (but there always was!). Sometimes my husband would catch us discussing these things in the middle of August! What can I say? We were holiday partners in crime. And it never felt too early to start planning for our favorite time of year.

One of the ways I honor the memory of my mom is by continuing with our holiday traditions and creating new ones I know she would have loved. I'm very thankful that I don't have to do this alone, because in addition to my wonderful pocket of friends, family, and neighbors, I get to share the holidays with *you*!

If there's one thing running my website has taught me over the years, it's that so many of you are just as passionate about the holidays as I am! Every November, my inbox explodes with requests for crowd-pleasing dinner ideas, cookie and candy recipes, entertaining tips, and all things cozy and festive. In fact, a couple of years ago the requests became so frequent that I began hosting a "Christmas in July" series on my website, which allows me to fulfill more recipe requests and share more holiday joy. But even with our annual summer tradition, I somehow never run out of recipes to share with you. (And I have endless notebooks filled with holiday recipe ideas to prove it!)

That is how this book came to be. It was inspired by all of you, and by our mutual love for the holidays! This shared passion is what gave me the drive and dedication needed to write this book. Because, just like you, I love filling the cookie jar, enjoying cocktails around the Christmas tree, hosting holiday pasta and movie nights, and creating cozy dinner parties for neighbors and friends. And this book is filled to the brim with ideas and recipes to keep your at-home holiday energy running high all season long.

Many of the recipes you'll find in this book are holiday classics, and I hope they'll become staples in your kitchen, and maybe even take root and become part of your holiday traditions! But, as in my childhood, there are plenty of unconventional recipes that might not be considered classic (yet!), but are totally delicious and guaranteed to be crowd-pleasers. In fact, it's the simple recipes that can be made spontaneously and don't require special-order ingredients—or days of prep—that are my favorites.

Some of my best holiday memories have been created with hungry people sharing a tray of baked ziti or a pot of soup, or a few sleepy friends catching up over coffee and cake. Sometimes it's those small moments—the ones that almost didn't happen—that end up being the best moments of all. So, whether you're planning on throwing one BIG bash, a series of smaller get-togethers, or bringing friends together for a cookie-baking bonanza, I hope these recipes will bring you comfort and joy this season—and for many seasons to come!

Cheers to being home for the holidays!

Ashley Manila

PART ONE

Holiday Party Menus

HOLIDAY MOVIE NIGHT/ GAME NIGHT

Ultimate Meatball Sliders | 47

Garlic Parmesan Popcorn | 55

Italian Hoagie Party Platter | 59

Holiday Sangria | 208

Rosemary Lemonade | 215

Peanut Butter M&M® Cookies | 176

Molasses Cream Pies | 171

ADDITIONAL SUGGESTED BEVERAGES: Water, sparkling water, beer

COOKIE BOX PARTY

Triple Chocolate Brownies | 159

My Favorite Butter Cookies | 154

Dark Chocolate & Sea Salt Caramels | 193

Lemon White Chocolate Macadamia Nut Cookies | 167

Chocolate-Covered Peanut Butter Christmas Trees | 186

Peppermint Bark | 201

Chocolate Crinkles | 168

Bourbon Butter Pecan Fudge | 185

SUGGESTED BEVERAGES: Milk and water for kids, sparkling water and dry prosecco for adults

FESTIVE COCKTAIL PARTY

Brie Bites with Cranberry Chutney | 60

Four-Cheese Spinach Dip | 66

Lemon-Rosemary Chicken Wings | 45

Candied Pecans | 103

Caramelized Onion Dip Snack Board | 51

Pomegranate Party Punch | 212

Cranberry-Ginger Moscow Mules | 216

Black Forest Cheesecake | 137

Chocolate-Covered Almond Toffee | 197

ADDITIONAL SUGGESTED BEVERAGES: Sparkling water, water, beer, red wine, white wine

BOOZY SUNDAY BRUNCH

Bloody Mary Brunch Bar | 220

Piña Colada Sunrise Mimosas | 223

Sugar & Spice Donuts | 31

Brown Butter–Orange Ricotta Pancakes | 16

Bacon & Caramelized Onion Quiche | 23

Rosemary & Garlic Roasted Potatoes | 94

ADDITIONAL SUGGESTED BEVERAGES: Freshly brewed coffee, orange juice

Holiday Party Menus | 7

FAMILY-STYLE FEAST

Caramelized Onion Dip Snack Board | 51

Italian Hoagie Party Platter | 59

Chicken Parmesan for a Crowd | 84

Crowd-Pleasing Caesar Salad with Garlic Bread Croutons | 111

Salted Caramel Apple Pie Bars | 173

Extra-Creamy Cannoli | 125

SUGGESTED BEVERAGES: Dry red wine, dry white wine, water

CHRISTMAS MORNING BREAKFAST

Fluffy Cinnamon Rolls | 19

Cranberry Orange Scones | 32

Cozy Mulled Cider | 219

Morning Glory Muffins | 39

Sausage & Potato Breakfast Casserole | 28

Cinnamon Apple French Toast | 35

ADDITIONAL SUGGESTED BEVERAGES: Freshly brewed coffee, orange juice, Champagne or dry prosecco

SPECIAL OCCASION SIT-DOWN DINNER

Feel-Good Holiday Salad | 103

Parker House Rolls | 98

Special Occasion Roast Beef with Roasted Carrots | 83

Mashed Potatoes | 90

Balsamic Roasted Brussels Sprouts with Pancetta & Pomegranate Seeds | 108

New York–Style Cheesecake with Grand Marnier® Cranberry Sauce | 121

Eggnog Tiramisu | 118

SUGGESTED BEVERAGES:
Red wine, prosecco or Champagne, water, sparkling water

NEW YEAR'S EVE DINNER

Whipped Ricotta Toast with Olives & Almonds | 42

Candied Pecans | 103

Prosciutto-Wrapped Jalapeño Poppers | 56

Mini Crab Cakes with Spicy Remoulade | 65

Lemon Risotto with Brown Butter Scallops | 79

Warm Bacon & Green Bean Salad | 115

Sparkling Champagne Cupcakes | 141

Triple Chocolate Brownies | 159

SUGGESTED BEVERAGES:
Champagne, white wine, red wine, beer, sparkling water, water, coffee

ITALIAN-INSPIRED SUNDAY SUPPER

Crowd-Pleasing Caesar Salad with Garlic Bread Croutons | 111

Italian Wedding Soup | 97

Rigatoni Bolognese with Garlic Bread | 87

Extra-Creamy Cannoli | 125

Cranberry-Pistachio Biscotti | 163

SUGGESTED BEVERAGES:
Bold Italian red wine, water, coffee

KID-FRIENDLY CROWD-PLEASERS

Creamy White Cheddar Macaroni & Cheese | 107

Ultimate Meatball Sliders | 47

Crowd-Pleasing Caesar Salad with Garlic Bread Croutons | 111

Meatball & Spinach Baked Ziti | 77

Christmas Funfetti Sheet Cake | 133

Peanut Butter M&M® Cookies | 176

Double Chocolate–Banana Bundt Cake | 36

SUGGESTED BEVERAGES:
Water, milk, flavored sparkling water

CHRISTMAS EVE FOR A CROWD

Lemon-Rosemary Chicken Wings | 45

Italian Hoagie Party Platter | 59

Caramelized Onion Dip Snack Board | 51

Pasta Fagioli | 104

Herb-Crusted Salmon with Mashed Potatoes | 90

Pan-Seared Cod in Lemon-Caper Sauce | 74

Eggnog Tiramisu | 118

Cranberry Cherry Pie | 145

Kahlúa Peppermint Mocha Chocolate Truffles | 190

SUGGESTED BEVERAGES:
Red wine, white wine, dry prosecco, sparkling water, water

CHRISTMAS DINNER

Mini Crab Cakes with Spicy Remoulade | 65

Brie Bites with Cranberry Chutney | 60

Feel-Good Holiday Salad | 103

Holiday Hens with Wild Rice Pilaf | 70

Parker House Rolls | 98

Chocolate Crinkles | 168

Gingerbread Celebration Cake | 149

Pumpkin Cheesecake with Pecan Praline Sauce | 129

SUGGESTED BEVERAGES:
Red wine, white wine, dry prosecco, water

PART TWO

The Recipes

CHAPTER

Breakfast & Brunch

If you're a breakfast person, this is the chapter for you! Get ready to dive into pancakes, muffins, and donuts galore. These are all holiday staples in our house, and they pair perfectly with lazy mornings, cozy pajamas, and freshly brewed coffee. But even if you're not in the breakfast fan club, I'm convinced this collection of sweet and savory recipes will quickly turn you into a morning person!

Brown Butter–Orange Ricotta Pancakes | 16

Fluffy Cinnamon Rolls | 19

Bacon & Caramelized Onion Quiche | 23

Nutella® Beignets | 25

Sausage & Potato Breakfast Casserole | 28

Sugar & Spice Donuts | 31

Cranberry Orange Scones | 32

Cinnamon Apple French Toast | 35

Double Chocolate–Banana Bundt Cake | 36

Morning Glory Muffins | 39

Brown Butter-Orange Ricotta Pancakes | SERVES 4

My husband loves pancakes, and I love making them for him! And while he's typically a flavor purist (his favorite ice cream flavor is vanilla), he went wild over these fluffy brown butter and orange flapjacks. The flavors are subtle and don't overwhelm your palate like chocolate—or even berries—can do sometimes. The addition of ricotta cheese makes them as light as air, while the brown butter and orange zest add just the right amount of flavor. And let's not forget about the bourbon maple syrup: I want to drizzle it on everything in my life, and I have a feeling you will, too. It's delicious on waffles, French toast, popovers . . . you name it!

RICOTTA PANCAKES

- 2 tablespoons (28 g) unsalted butter, plus more for the pan
- 2 cups (240 g) all-purpose flour
- ¼ cup (50 g) granulated sugar
- 2 teaspoons baking powder
- ½ teaspoon baking soda
- ¼ teaspoon salt
- 2 large eggs, room temperature
- 1⅓ cups (302 ml) buttermilk, room temperature
- 8 ounces (227 g) whole-milk ricotta cheese, room temperature
- ¼ cup (57 ml) fresh orange juice
- 1½ tablespoons (18 g) finely grated orange zest
- 2 teaspoons pure vanilla extract

BOURBON MAPLE SYRUP

- 1½ cups (468 ml) pure maple syrup
- 1 tablespoon (14 ml) bourbon
- 1 teaspoon pure vanilla extract
- 2 tablespoons (28 ml) fresh orange juice

FOR THE PANCAKES

1. In a small saucepan over medium heat, melt the butter. Continue cooking, swirling the pan occasionally, until golden brown in color, about 5 minutes. Remove the pan from the heat and scrape the butter into a small bowl. Set aside.
2. In a large bowl, whisk together the flour, sugar, baking powder, baking soda, and salt. Set aside.
3. In another large bowl, add the eggs and lightly beat them with a whisk. Add the buttermilk, ricotta, orange juice, orange zest, and vanilla and beat until well combined. Stir the buttermilk mixture into the flour mixture, mixing just until combined. Fold in the browned butter, stirring just until evenly combined.
4. Heat a large cast-iron skillet or nonstick pan over medium-high heat. Add a tablespoon of butter to the pan and let it melt completely. Pour ¼ cup (70 ml) of batter into the skillet, then reduce the heat to medium. (Note: cook the batter in small batches so the pancakes don't blend together.)
5. Cook for 2 to 3 minutes, or until small bubbles form on top of the pancakes, then carefully flip and continue to cook until golden brown, about 2 to 3 more minutes. Repeat with the remaining batter, adding more butter to the pan as needed. Don't skimp on the butter! A well-greased pan is the key to crispy, golden-brown pancakes.
6. Serve pancakes warm with the bourbon maple syrup.

FOR THE SYRUP

1. In a small saucepan over medium heat, combine the maple syrup, bourbon, and vanilla.
2. Bring to a gentle simmer. Remove the pan from the heat and whisk in the orange juice. Use right away.

ASHLEY'S TIP

Cooked pancakes can be kept warm for up to 30 minutes. Preheat the oven to 175°F. Place a wire rack on top of a large baking sheet, then place the baking sheet in the oven. Place cooked pancakes on top of the rack to keep them warm as you cook the remaining batter. Carefully remove the pan from the oven and serve.

Fluffy Cinnamon Rolls | YIELDS 12 ROLLS

Who can resist a pan of warm and gooey cinnamon rolls? Not me! And not anyone I know. They're textbook comfort food and a Christmas morning tradition in our house. Just thinking about them instantly floods me with warmth and childhood nostalgia. Making them is a labor of love, but they're totally worth it . . . pinky promise!

CINNAMON ROLLS

- 1 (0.25-ounce/7-g) packet active dry yeast
- ¼ cup (57 ml) warm water (between 115° and 120°F)
- 3 cups (360 g) all-purpose flour
- ¼ cup (50 g) granulated sugar
- ½ teaspoon salt
- ¾ cup (170 ml) whole milk
- 5 tablespoons (70 ml) unsalted butter, melted
- 1 large egg, room temperature
- 1 teaspoon pure vanilla extract
- Nonstick baking spray

FILLING

- 1 stick (113 g) unsalted butter, room temperature
- 1 cup (213 g) packed light brown sugar
- 1 tablespoon (5 g) ground cinnamon

CREAM CHEESE GLAZE

- 4 ounces (113 g) full-fat cream cheese, room temperature
- 1 tablespoon (14 ml) whole milk
- 1 teaspoon pure vanilla extract
- 1 cup (114 g) confectioners' sugar, sifted
- ¼ teaspoon salt

FOR THE CINNAMON ROLLS

1. In a small bowl, sprinkle the yeast over the water and set it aside until it bubbles up, about 5 minutes.
2. In the bowl of an electric stand mixer, combine the flour, sugar, and salt, and whisk well by hand to combine.
3. In a medium bowl, whisk together the milk, melted butter, egg, and vanilla, beating until well combined.
4. Pour the wet ingredients and yeast mixture into the dry ingredients, and, using a rubber spatula, stir together to form a rough dough.
5. Place the bowl on the stand mixer and attach the dough hook. With the mixer on medium speed, knead the dough for 10 minutes, or until the dough is smooth and pulls away from the bottom and sides of the bowl.
6. Cover the bowl tightly with plastic wrap and set aside for 1 hour, or until it's doubled in size.
7. Turn the dough out onto a lightly floured work surface. Sprinkle a little flour on top, and using a rolling pin, roll it into a 12 x 18-inch rectangle.

FOR THE FILLING

1. Cut the butter into ½-inch cubes. Place in a small bowl to soften.
2. In a medium bowl, combine the brown sugar and cinnamon until well combined.

FOR THE GLAZE

1. In the bowl of a stand mixer fitted with the paddle attachment, or in a large bowl using a handheld electric mixer, beat the cream cheese on medium speed until smooth. Add the milk and vanilla and beat until combined.
2. Reduce the mixer speed to low and gradually add the confectioners' sugar. Add the salt. Once the ingredients are incorporated, increase the speed to medium-high and beat for 1 minute, or until smooth and creamy.

TO ASSEMBLE AND BAKE

1. Preheat the oven to 350°F. Lightly grease the sides and bottom of a 9 x 13-inch baking pan with nonstick baking spray and set it aside.
2. Using a small metal spatula, spread the softened butter evenly over the dough, leaving a ¼-inch border along the edges. Sprinkle evenly with the brown sugar mixture.

continues on p. 20

3. Starting from the long edge closest to you, roll the dough into a log, jellyroll style, keeping it as tight as possible while rolling. (Note: The tighter the roll, the less filling that will leak out during baking.)

4. Score the dough lightly into 12 equal pieces. Cut the dough at the score marks. The easiest way to do this is to slide a long piece of unflavored dental floss under the dough. Wrap it up around the score mark, and then pull the two sides tightly in opposite directions to pull the floss through the roll. Repeat for all rolls.

5. Carefully arrange the rolls in the prepared pan, making four rows of three rolls, and leaving about 2 inches between each row of rolls.

6. Tightly cover the pan with plastic wrap and set it aside to rise for 1 hour, or until the rolls have puffed up in the pan and have almost doubled in size. Remove the plastic wrap.

7. Bake for 25 to 30 minutes, or until puffed up and golden brown. (Note: If you use a glass or ceramic baking pan, you may need to increase the baking time by 5 to 10 minutes.)

8. Remove the pan from the oven and place on a wire rack to cool for 5 minutes. Then slowly spread the warm rolls with the cream cheese frosting. Serve warm.

ASHLEY'S TIP

To partially prepare in advance, follow the directions in "To Assemble and Bake" up to step 6, but instead of setting the rolls aside, place them in the refrigerator, up to 12 hours. Before you plan on baking, remove the pan from the fridge and let the rolls rise at room temperature until they've almost doubled in size, about 2 hours. Then remove the plastic wrap, preheat the oven, and follow the directions starting at step 7.

Bacon & Caramelized Onion Quiche | YIELDS ONE 10-INCH QUICHE

This quiche combines two of my all-time favorite ingredients: bacon and caramelized onions! But the deliciousness doesn't stop there . . . the filling is enriched with Gruyère cheese, fresh thyme, and plenty of spices. And let's not forget about the all-butter crust—flaky, buttery, and spiked with fresh thyme leaves for the perfect pop of flavor. This is such a lovely addition to any brunch menu, and it gets bonus points because leftovers can be enjoyed for lunch or dinner for days to come.

CRUST

- 2½ cups (300 g) all-purpose flour
- 1½ teaspoons finely chopped fresh thyme leaves
- 1 teaspoon granulated sugar
- ½ teaspoon salt
- 2 sticks (227 g) very cold unsalted butter, cut into ½-inch cubes
- ½ cup (113 ml) ice water (you may not use it all)

BACON & CARAMELIZED ONION FILLING

- 2 tablespoons (28 g) unsalted butter, plus more for greasing
- 6 large (920 g) yellow onions, cut in half and thinly sliced
- 1½ tablespoons (21 ml) water
- 1½ teaspoons finely chopped fresh thyme leaves
- 1 teaspoon packed light brown sugar
- 8 ounces (227 g) sliced bacon
- 3 large eggs, room temperature
- ¾ cup (170 ml) heavy cream, room temperature
- ¼ teaspoon fine sea salt
- ¼ teaspoon freshly ground black pepper
- ⅛ teaspoon cayenne pepper
- ⅛ teaspoon ground nutmeg
- 2 teaspoons country Dijon mustard
- 4 ounces (113 g) Gruyère cheese, coarsely grated
- Sprigs of fresh thyme, for garnish

FOR THE CRUST

1. In a large bowl, whisk together the flour, thyme, sugar, and salt. Add the cubed butter and toss with the flour to coat.

2. Using a pastry cutter, work the butter into the flour until the mixture resembles a coarse meal. The bits of butter should be about the size of peas.

3. Using a rubber spatula, slowly incorporate just enough ice water (start with ⅓ cup/75 ml) to form moist clumps, adding more water as needed.

4. Pour the shaggy dough out onto a clean surface and knead it gently, until it comes together in a ball. (Note: The less water you add, the flakier your crust will be. Try to knead it together without additional water, and add a small amount *only* if absolutely needed.)

5. Form the dough into a neat ball and gently flatten into a disk.

6. Wrap the disk in plastic wrap and place in the refrigerator to chill for at least 2 hours or up to 24 hours.

FOR THE FILLING

1. Preheat the oven to 350°F. Lightly grease a 10-inch ceramic quiche pan with butter. Set it aside.

2. In a large sauté pan over medium heat, melt the butter. Add the onions and cook, stirring occasionally, for 10 minutes. Reduce the heat to medium-low, and stir in the water, thyme, and brown sugar. Continue cooking, stirring occasionally, for 30 minutes, or until the onions are soft and caramelized. If at any point the onions look too dry, add a teaspoon or two of water to the skillet. (Note: The onions may be caramelized up to 24 hours in advance. Cool completely and place in an airtight container in the refrigerator until needed.)

3. In the meantime, warm a large cast-iron skillet over medium heat. Add the bacon and cook, turning occasionally, until crisp and fully cooked, 6 to 7 minutes. Transfer the bacon to a paper towel–lined plate to cool. Then transfer the bacon to a cutting board and roughly chop. Set the bacon aside.

4. In a medium bowl, combine the eggs, cream, salt, black pepper, cayenne pepper, and nutmeg. Whisk vigorously until well combined. Set the egg mixture aside.

continues on p. 24

5. Remove the crust from the refrigerator and let it rest for 15 minutes. Lightly flour a rolling pin and a large clean work surface.

6. Set the dough in the middle of the work surface and, beginning from the center of the disk, roll the dough away from you in one firm and even stroke. After each stroke, rotate the disk a quarter turn clockwise and roll again. Lightly sprinkle more flour on the surface, dough, or rolling pin as needed. Use just enough to prevent the dough from sticking. As the disk of dough becomes larger, avoid overstretching the center of the dough. Continue rolling until the dough is about 16 inches in diameter and ¼ inch in thickness.

7. Place the crust into the prepared pan, and gently press it into the bottom and ridges.

8. Trim excess dough, leaving ½ inch of overhang. Roll the overhang under the rim of the pie plate and crimp. Refrigerate for 15 minutes.

9. Remove the crust from the fridge. Line the crust with parchment paper and fill with pie weights or dry beans. Bake in the lower third of the oven for 25 minutes.

10. Remove the crust from the oven. Carefully remove the pie weights and parchment paper and prick the bottom of the crust all over with a fork. Return the crust to the oven and bake for 15 more minutes. Cool the crust on a wire rack for 10 minutes.

11. Carefully spread the Dijon mustard in a thin layer across the crust, then top with three-quarters of the onions and half of the bacon.

12. Pour the eggs over the onions and bacon, then sprinkle with the Gruyère. Top with the remaining onions and bacon.

13. Bake for 40 minutes, or until the crust is golden brown and the filling is set.

14. Cool the quiche on a wire rack for 15 minutes. Sprinkle with thyme sprigs, slice, and serve warm.

Nutella® Beignets | YIELDS ABOUT 24 BEIGNETS

New Orleans is one of my favorite cities in the entire world. My husband and I visit as often as we can, and we always make time in our schedule for multiple beignet pit stops! If you've never had a beignet, don't be put off by their fancy name. In their simplest form, they're just squares of fried dough sprinkled with confectioners' sugar. So simple but so delicious! However, in my travels I've seen everything from crab cake beignets to apple pie beignets. My spin on the classic? Nutella®-stuffed beignets covered in crunchy cinnamon sugar! We love these for breakfast, but they can easily double as dessert. I'll leave that up to you . . .

1½ cups (340 ml) warm water (between 115° and 120°F)

2¼ cups (447 g) granulated sugar, divided

1 (0.25-ounce/7-g) packet active dry yeast

2 large eggs, room temperature

1 cup (227 ml) evaporated milk

1 tablespoon (14 ml) pure vanilla extract

7½ cups (900 g) bread flour, divided

¼ teaspoon ground nutmeg

5 tablespoons (71 g) unsalted butter, cut into ½-inch cubes, room temperature

1½ teaspoons salt

2 tablespoons (14 g) ground cinnamon

2 cups (596 g) Nutella® or another chocolate-hazelnut spread

5 cups (992 ml) peanut oil, for deep-frying

1. In a medium bowl, combine the water, ¾ cup (149 g) of the sugar, and the yeast, and whisk well to combine. Set the bowl aside until the mixture bubbles up and has become foamy, about 10 minutes.
2. In the bowl of an electric stand mixer, whisk the eggs until well combined. Add the evaporated milk and vanilla and whisk by hand to combine.
3. Add 4 cups (480 g) of the flour and the nutmeg and using a rubber spatula, stir together to form a shaggy dough.
4. Place the bowl on the stand mixer and attach the dough hook. With the mixer on medium speed, knead until a smooth dough forms, about 2 minutes.
5. Reduce the speed to low and slowly pour in the yeast mixture—take care when adding, as it will splash up if added too quickly. Beat the mixture until smooth.
6. Add the butter and beat until completely incorporated.
7. Finally, add in the remaining 3½ cups (420 g) of flour and the salt. Beat until the dough is smooth and cohesive, about 2 minutes.
8. Cover the bowl tightly with plastic wrap and refrigerate the dough for at least 2½ hours, or overnight.
9. In a large bowl, combine the remaining 1½ cups (298 g) sugar and the cinnamon. Set the bowl aside.
10. Scrape the Nutella® into a medium piping bag with a small open tip and set it aside.
11. When you're ready to fry, line a large rimmed baking sheet with three layers of paper towels and set it aside.
12. In a large pot (at least 6-inches deep), heat the oil to between 355° and 360°F.
13. Remove the dough from the refrigerator. Scrape the dough onto a lightly floured surface and roll out into a ¼-inch-thick rectangle. Using a pizza cutter, cut the dough into 2½-inch squares.

continues on p. 27

14. In batches, fry the pieces of dough until they puff up and are golden brown in color, about 1 minute per side.

15. Using a large slotted spoon or fish spatula, transfer the beignets to the prepared baking sheet. As soon as the beignets are cool enough to handle, generously coat them in the cinnamon-sugar mixture. (Do this while they're still warm so the coating sticks.)

16. Once all the beignets have been coated, you're ready to fill them with Nutella®! To do this, poke a small hole in the side of each beignet using a straw or the end of a spoon. Insert the nozzle of the piping bag into the hole and gently press to fill. Don't squeeze too firmly, or the beignet will tear open—go slowly.

17. Place on a large serving platter and serve warm, with plenty of napkins!

ASHLEY'S TIP

You'll need a candy thermometer for this recipe. Be sure to keep your working oil temperature between 355° and 360°F. You may need to wait a few minutes between batches to get the oil back to this range to avoid burned or soggy beignets. An enameled cast iron pot will maintain the oil temperature best.

Sausage & Potato Breakfast Casserole | SERVES 6 TO 8

Looking for the easiest way to make eggs for a crowd? Say hello to breakfast casserole! Sure, it's not the sexiest-sounding dish. (I mean, anything with the word "casserole" in it rarely is!) But what it lacks in title appeal, it more than makes up for in taste. Even toddlers and teens dig this recipe. You can serve it with bagels, tortillas, or toasted English muffins on the side, and let your guests make their own breakfast sandwiches. Or simply slice into squares and serve directly from the pan.

Nonstick cooking spray

1 large russet potato (255 g), peeled and cut into ¼-inch cubes

3 tablespoons (42 ml) olive oil, divided

1 pound (454 g) sweet Italian sausage, casings removed

1 large red bell pepper (260 g), seeds removed, diced

1 large green bell pepper (260 g), seeds removed, diced

1 small red onion (165 g), diced

4 cloves garlic, minced

2 tablespoons (20 g) fresh rosemary leaves, finely chopped

1 teaspoon Italian seasoning

¾ teaspoon salt

½ teaspoon freshly ground black pepper

3 cups (about 130 g) packed baby spinach

12 large eggs, room temperature

1½ cups (170 g) coarsely grated sharp cheddar cheese

½ cup (57 g) finely grated Parmesan cheese

½ cup (113 ml) whole milk, room temperature

¼ cup (43 g) thinly sliced scallions, green part only, for garnish

1. Preheat the oven to 350°F. Lightly grease a 9 x 13-inch baking dish with nonstick cooking spray. Set it aside.
2. Bring a medium saucepan of water to a rolling boil. Add the potato and cook for 5 minutes. Quickly drain and rinse under cold water. Place the strainer over a bowl to drain excess liquid and set it aside.
3. Line a large plate with several layers of paper towels and set it aside.
4. Place a large skillet over medium heat. Add 1 tablespoon (14 ml) of the oil.
5. Add the sausage to the skillet and, using a wooden spoon, break the sausage up into small chunks. Cook until browned and no pink remains, 5 to 6 minutes.
6. Using a slotted spoon, transfer the sausage to a clean plate and set it aside. Carefully drain any excess grease from the skillet and then return the skillet to the burner.
7. Add the remaining 2 tablespoons (28 ml) of oil to the skillet, and then add the bell peppers and onion, and cook until the vegetables begin to soften, about 5 minutes.
8. Stir in the garlic, rosemary, Italian seasoning, salt, and black pepper and continue cooking for another 2 minutes. Stir in the spinach and cook for 1 minute, just until it begins to wilt.
9. Remove the skillet from the heat and, using a large slotted spoon, transfer the vegetables to the paper towel-lined plate to absorb any excess liquid (so the casserole won't be soggy). Set the vegetables aside.
10. In a large bowl, whisk together the eggs, both cheeses, and milk, beating until well combined.
11. Spread half of the potatoes, half of the veggie mixture, and half of the sausage on the bottom of the prepared baking dish. Top with all the egg mixture, then repeat with the remaining potatoes, veggies, and sausage.
12. Bake the casserole, uncovered, for 45 to 50 minutes, or until completely set in the middle and the top is a deep golden brown. (If the top is getting too brown, cover the pan with foil and continue baking until done, checking it every 15 minutes or so.)
13. Place the casserole on a wire rack to cool for 20 minutes before slicing and serving. Garnish with the scallions right before serving.

ASHLEY'S TIP

You can make and assemble this recipe up to step 11, then cover tightly with plastic wrap and place in the refrigerator for up to 12 hours. Before baking, preheat the oven, remove the plastic wrap, and follow the directions starting with step 12.

Sugar & Spice Donuts | YIELDS 12 DONUTS

Sugar and spice and everything nice . . . I can't think of a more perfect way to describe these donuts! Made with brown butter and comforting spices, these donuts are on regular rotation in our household—and not just during the holidays! They bake up in less than fifteen minutes and are the perfect treat for mornings when you want something delicious but need it on the fly! You'll need a donut pan for this recipe, but I promise it's a worthwhile investment!

BROWN BUTTER DONUTS

Nonstick baking spray

6 tablespoons (85 g) unsalted butter

2⅔ cups (320 g) all-purpose flour

2½ teaspoons baking powder

½ teaspoon salt

¼ teaspoon ground nutmeg

¼ teaspoon ground cinnamon

½ cup (106 g) packed light brown sugar

½ cup (99 g) granulated sugar

2 large eggs, room temperature

1 tablespoon (14 ml) pure vanilla extract

1 cup (227 g) full-fat sour cream, room temperature

CINNAMON-SUGAR COATING

1 stick (113 g) unsalted butter

1½ cups (298 g) granulated sugar

2½ teaspoons ground cinnamon

½ teaspoon ground nutmeg

½ teaspoon ground ginger

½ teaspoon ground allspice

FOR THE DONUTS

1. Preheat the oven to 350°F. Generously grease two 6-mold donut pans with nonstick baking spray and set the pans aside.

2. In a small saucepan over medium heat, melt the butter. Continue cooking, swirling the pan occasionally, until golden brown in color, about 5 minutes. Remove the pan from the heat and scrape the butter into a small bowl. Set the bowl aside.

3. In a large bowl, combine the flour, baking powder, salt, nutmeg, and cinnamon. Set the bowl aside.

4. In another large bowl, whisk together the browned butter and both sugars, beating until well combined. Beat in the eggs, one at a time, then whisk in the vanilla. Using a rubber spatula, fold in the sour cream.

5. Gently fold the dry ingredients into the egg mixture, mixing until just combined.

6. Scrape the batter into a large piping bag. Pipe the batter into the prepared pans, dividing evenly among the molds, about 75 g/ 3 tablespoons batter per mold. (Note: You only need a small swirl of batter per mold, as they will spread and puff up in the oven.)

7. Bake for 12 minutes, or until the donuts spring back when lightly pressed.

8. Allow the donuts to cool in the pan for 5 minutes before gently unmolding them and transferring them to a wire rack.

FOR THE COATING

1. In a small saucepan over medium heat, melt the butter. Continue cooking, swirling the pan occasionally, until golden brown in color, about 5 minutes. Remove the pan from the heat and scrape the butter into a wide, shallow bowl. Set the bowl aside.

2. In another wide, shallow bowl combine the sugar and spices. Set the bowl aside.

TO ASSEMBLE

1. When the donuts are cool enough to handle, dip them in the melted butter, being sure to coat both sides and the edges.

2. Roll the donuts in the cinnamon-sugar mixture, generously coating the entire surface. Serve at once!

ASHLEY'S TIP

Donuts are best served the day they are baked, but will keep, wrapped tightly in plastic wrap, for up to 24 hours.

Cranberry Orange Scones | YIELDS 8 SCONES

My favorite thing about scones is what used to be my least favorite thing about scones. I know that's confusing, so I'll explain. Once upon a time, I had a strong distaste for scones and thought they were easily the world's most boring baked good. But at some point in my baking career, I decided to give them another shot and discovered that just because scones can be boring, doesn't mean they have to be. In fact, when made correctly, scones are flaky, buttery, and an absolute treat. My holiday-inspired version features a delightful combination of fresh cranberries and festive flavors, plus a sticky-sweet orange glaze! The colors and flavors are so bright and happy, and they're always a huge hit, even with "scone haters." Serve with coffee and tea and get ready for folks to ask you for the recipe.

CRANBERRY ORANGE SCONES

- 3 cups plus 2 tablespoons (375 g) all-purpose flour, divided, plus more for dusting
- 1 tablespoon (14 g) baking powder
- ⅓ cup (67 g) granulated sugar
- ¼ cup (53 g) packed light brown sugar
- ½ teaspoon salt
- ½ teaspoon ground cinnamon
- ¼ teaspoon ground cardamom
- 1 stick (113 g) unsalted butter, very cold, cut into ½-inch cubes
- ¾ cup (170 ml) heavy cream, cold
- 1 large egg, cold
- 1½ tablespoons (18 g) finely grated orange zest
- 2 teaspoons pure vanilla extract
- ½ teaspoon orange extract
- 2 cups (198 g) fresh or frozen cranberries, roughly chopped (if frozen, do not thaw)
- 1 large egg, beaten
- 1 teaspoon water
- 3 tablespoons (42 g) sparkling sugar

ORANGE GLAZE

- 1½ cups (170 g) confectioners' sugar, sifted
- 2 tablespoons (28 ml) fresh orange juice, plus more as needed
- 1 teaspoon finely grated orange zest
- ½ teaspoon pure vanilla extract
- ⅛ teaspoon salt

FOR THE SCONES

1. Preheat the oven to 425°F. Line a large baking sheet with parchment paper and set it aside.
2. In a large bowl, combine 3 cups (360 g) of the flour, the baking powder, both sugars, salt, cinnamon, and cardamom. Mix well to combine.
3. Add the cubed butter and toss with the flour to coat. Using a pastry cutter, work the butter into the flour until the mixture resembles a coarse meal. The bits of butter should be about the size of peas.
4. In a glass measuring cup, whisk together the cream, cold egg, orange zest, vanilla, and orange extract.
5. In a medium bowl, combine the cranberries and the remaining 2 tablespoons (15 g) of flour, tossing well to coat the cranberries in the flour.
6. Pour the cream mixture into the center of the flour mixture. Then add the flour-coated cranberries. Using a rubber spatula, stir everything together until just moistened. (Don't worry if the dough looks shaggy!)
7. Empty the dough out onto a clean, lightly floured work surface. Knead the dough until it comes together, 8 to 10 times, then shape it into an 8-inch disk.
8. Cut the disk into 8 wedges and carefully transfer them to the prepared baking sheet, leaving 2 inches between each wedge.
9. In a small bowl, whisk together the beaten egg and water until well combined. Lightly brush the top of each scone with the egg wash. Then sprinkle generously with sparkling sugar.
10. Bake for 20 to 22 minutes, or until golden brown. Allow the scones to cool for 10 minutes on the baking sheet before glazing.

FOR THE GLAZE

1. In a small bowl, combine the confectioners' sugar, orange juice, orange zest, vanilla, and salt; whisk until well combined. If the glaze appears too thick, add a little more orange juice. If the glaze appears too thin, add a small amount of confectioners' sugar. It should be very thick but pourable.
2. Drizzle the glaze over the scones and serve at once.

Cinnamon Apple French Toast | SERVES 4

Apple pie French toast... need I say more? This brunch recipe is make-ahead friendly and as it bakes, it makes your home smell better than any scented candle ever will! The toast itself bakes up crisp yet tender, with caramelized edges. And the cinnamon apple syrup is essentially apple pie filling on top of your French toast. My favorite apples to use for this recipe are Honeycrisp, Gala, or Cortland. But Granny Smith and Golden Delicious work great, too.

FRENCH TOAST

¾ cup (170 ml) whole milk

¾ cup (170 ml) heavy cream

7 large eggs plus 2 egg yolks, room temperature

2 tablespoons (28 ml) rum or bourbon (optional)

1 tablespoon (14 ml) pure vanilla extract

1 loaf crusty French bread or sourdough, cut into 8 (1-inch) slices

6 tablespoons (85 g) unsalted butter

1 cup (213 g) packed light brown sugar

½ cup (156 ml) pure maple syrup

½ teaspoon ground cinnamon

¼ teaspoon salt

¼ teaspoon ground nutmeg

⅛ teaspoon allspice

CINNAMON APPLE SYRUP

5 large apples, peeled, cored, and cut into ¼-inch-thick slices

2 teaspoons fresh lemon juice

4 tablespoons (57 g) unsalted butter

¼ teaspoon salt

¼ cup (50 g) granulated sugar

¼ cup (53 g) packed light brown sugar

1 tablespoon (14 ml) rum or bourbon (optional)

1 tablespoon (11 g) cornstarch

1¼ teaspoons ground cinnamon

⅛ teaspoon ground nutmeg

⅛ teaspoon ground allspice

1 pint butter pecan ice cream, for serving (optional)

FOR THE FRENCH TOAST

1. In a large bowl, combine the milk, cream, eggs, egg yolks, rum or bourbon (if using), and vanilla. Whisk well to combine and set the egg mixture aside.

2. Arrange the bread in a 9 x 13-inch baking dish. Pour the egg mixture over the bread, making sure both sides of each piece are well coated. Wrap the dish tightly with plastic wrap and refrigerate for at least 6 hours, or overnight.

3. Thirty minutes before you're ready to bake, preheat the oven to 350°F.

4. In a small saucepan over medium heat, melt the butter. Remove the pan from the heat and whisk in the brown sugar, maple syrup, cinnamon, salt, nutmeg, and allspice.

5. Spread this mixture evenly across the bottom of a second 9 x 13-inch baking dish. Carefully arrange the soaked bread on top, leaving any excess liquid behind.

6. Bake the French toast for 35 minutes, or until the bread is golden brown and the syrup mixture is bubbling. While it bakes, make the cinnamon apple syrup!

FOR THE SYRUP

1. In a large bowl, combine the apples with the lemon juice and toss well to coat. Set the bowl aside.

2. In a large saucepan over medium heat, melt the butter. Add the apples, salt, and both sugars. Using a wooden spoon, mix well to combine. Cook, stirring occasionally, until the apples have softened, 8 to 10 minutes.

3. Add the rum or bourbon (if using), cornstarch, cinnamon, nutmeg, and allspice and mix well to combine. Continue cooking for 4 to 5 minutes, stirring occasionally, until the mixture thickens. Remove the pan from the heat.

TO ASSEMBLE

1. Place one or two pieces of the French toast on a serving plate, top with a generous amount of the cinnamon apple syrup and, if desired, a scoop (or two!) of butter pecan ice cream. Serve warm.

Double Chocolate–Banana Bundt Cake | YIELDS 1 CAKE

Cake for breakfast? You better believe it! That's the magic of baking cake in a Bundt pan ... it instantly turns it into a breakfast option. (At least in our house it does!) This "breakfast cake" is super chocolatey and has just the right amount of banana flavor. Be sure to use overripe bananas, which create the insanely moist texture this cake is known for.

CHOCOLATE-BANANA BUNDT CAKE

Nonstick baking spray

2 cups (240 g) all-purpose flour

1 cup (85 g) Dutch-process cocoa powder

2¼ teaspoons baking powder

1 teaspoon espresso powder

½ teaspoon salt

½ teaspoon ground cinnamon

2 sticks (227g) unsalted butter, room temperature

1¾ cups (349 g) granulated sugar

1 cup (213 g) packed light brown sugar

4 large eggs, room temperature

2 teaspoons pure vanilla extract

3 bananas (325 g), very ripe, mashed well

½ cup (113 g) sour cream, room temperature

¼ cup (50 ml) vegetable oil

¼ cup (57 ml) boiling water

CHOCOLATE GLAZE

3.5 ounces (100 g) semisweet chocolate, finely chopped

½ cup (113 ml) heavy cream

1 teaspoon pure vanilla extract

FOR THE CAKE

1. Preheat the oven to 325°F. Generously grease a 10-cup Bundt cake pan with nonstick baking spray. Set it aside.

2. In a large bowl, sift together the flour, cocoa powder, baking powder, espresso powder, salt, and cinnamon. Set it aside.

3. In the bowl of a stand mixer fitted with the paddle attachment, or in a large bowl using a handheld electric mixer, beat the butter at medium speed until smooth and creamy, about 1 minute.

4. Gradually add both sugars, turning the mixer off occasionally to scrape down the sides and bottom of the bowl. Once all sugar has been added, increase the speed to medium-high and beat until light and fluffy, about 3 minutes.

5. Reduce the mixer to medium speed and beat in the eggs one at a time, beating well after each addition, and scraping the bottom and sides of the bowl as needed.

6. In a large glass measuring cup, combine the vanilla, bananas, sour cream, and oil and mix well.

7. With the mixer on low speed, add the dry ingredients into the butter mixture, adding it in three additions, alternating with the banana mixture in two additions, beginning and ending with the dry ingredients. Mix until just combined.

8. Pour in the hot water and let it stand for 1 minute, then use a rubber spatula to gently fold it into the mixture until evenly combined.

9. Scrape the batter into the prepared pan and smooth the top. Bake for 68 to 70 minutes, or until a toothpick or cake tester inserted in the center of the cake comes out clean.

10. Place the pan on a wire rack to cool for 15 minutes. Then invert the cake onto the rack and cool completely, about 2 hours.

FOR THE GLAZE

1. Place the chocolate in a small heatproof bowl and set it aside.

2. In a small saucepan over medium heat, warm the cream until it comes to a steady simmer. Pour over the chocolate and let it sit for 1 minute, then whisk until smooth. Whisk in the vanilla.

3. Slowly spoon the glaze over the cooled cake, letting it drip down the sides. Allow the glaze to set for at least 1 hour before slicing and serving.

Morning Glory Muffins | YIELDS 12 MUFFINS

These delicious muffins are rumored to have originated on Nantucket Island, which just so happens to be my favorite place in the whole world! My husband proposed to me there, and we've created some of our most cherished memories on that little slice of paradise. Sadly, the Morning Glory Cafe, where the recipe originated, closed long before our yearly visits. But over time, morning glory muffins have gained in popularity and are now sold in plenty of bakeries on and off the island. Packed with carrots, dried and fresh fruit, coconut, and crunchy nuts, these muffins are big on flavor and texture!

¾ cup (159 g) packed light brown sugar

¼ cup (50 g) granulated sugar

3 large eggs, room temperature

1 cup (227 ml) coconut oil (refined or unrefined), melted and slightly cooled

1 tablespoon (14 ml) pure vanilla extract

2¾ cups (330 g) all-purpose flour

1 tablespoon (14 g) baking powder

2 teaspoons ground cinnamon

½ teaspoon ground ginger

½ teaspoon salt

2 cups (199 g) coarsely grated carrot (about 3 medium)

1 large Honeycrisp apple, coarsely grated (about 155 g)

1 small firm Bosc pear, coarsely grated (about 115 g)

1 cup (113 g) dried cranberries

1 cup (86 g) shredded sweetened coconut

½ cup (57 g) finely chopped walnuts or pecans

2½ tablespoons (35 ml) fresh orange juice

1. Preheat the oven to 400°F. Line a 12-cup regular muffin tin with paper liners. Set the muffin tin aside.

2. In a large bowl, whisk together both sugars, the eggs, coconut oil, and vanilla. Set bowl aside.

3. In a medium bowl, whisk together the flour, baking powder, cinnamon, ginger, and salt. Using a rubber spatula, fold the dry ingredients into the wet ingredients, mixing until just combined.

4. Fold in the carrot, apple, pear, cranberries, coconut, nuts, and orange juice, mixing just until combined.

5. Divide the batter evenly among the prepared muffin tin cups, filling them all the way up to the top. Don't worry if the batter overfills the liners.

6. Bake for 10 minutes, then reduce the oven to 375°F and continue baking for 14 to 15 minutes, or until the centers have puffed up and a toothpick inserted in the center of a muffin comes out clean or with a few moist crumbs attached.

7. Place the pan on a wire rack to cool for 10 minutes. Serve warm or at room temperature.

CHAPTER 2

Appetizers & Snacks

Your guests will swoon over these perfectly indulgent party bites. This chapter includes recipes that are a delicious way to kick off any event . . . but don't be surprised if you catch yourself making them even when you're not hosting a party.

Whipped Ricotta Toast with Olives & Almonds | 42

Lemon-Rosemary Chicken Wings | 45

Ultimate Meatball Sliders | 47

Caramelized Onion Dip Snack Board | 51

Garlic Parmesan Popcorn | 55

Prosciutto-Wrapped Jalapeño Poppers | 56

Italian Hoagie Party Platter | 59

Brie Bites with Cranberry Chutney | 60

Mini Crab Cakes with Spicy Remoulade | 65

Four-Cheese Spinach Dip | 66

Whipped Ricotta Toast with Olives & Almonds | YIELDS 8 TOASTS

Ricotta cheese is delicious as is . . . but when you whip it, something magical happens! It transforms into a silky-smooth blank canvas that's perfect for adding even more flavor. The magical trio of fresh thyme, orange zest, and honey enriches the sweet ricotta, while a scattering of green olives and toasted almonds creates balance and adds the perfect amount of crunch.

OLIVES & ALMONDS

¾ cup (89 g) raw almonds, roughly chopped

¼ cup (50 ml) olive oil

1½ tablespoons (18 g) finely grated orange zest

1 tablespoon (10 g) finely chopped fresh thyme leaves

¼ teaspoon flaky sea salt, crushed with your fingertips

1½ cups (240 g) pitted Castelvetrano olives, drained and roughly chopped

WHIPPED RICOTTA

15 ounces (425 g) whole milk ricotta cheese

2 tablespoons (28 ml) heavy cream

½ teaspoon fine sea salt

TOAST

1 crusty loaf sourdough bread (1 pound/454 g), cut into 8 (1-inch) slices

⅓ cup (67 ml) olive oil

FOR SERVING

½ teaspoon flaky sea salt

½ teaspoon freshly ground black pepper

¼ cup (85 ml) honey

Sprigs of fresh thyme, for garnish

FOR THE OLIVES & ALMONDS

1. In a medium skillet over medium-low heat, combine the almonds and oil and cook, stirring frequently, until the oil is sizzling and the almonds are fragrant, 3 to 4 minutes. Watch carefully to ensure they don't burn.

2. Remove the pan from the heat. Place a fine-mesh strainer on top of a small bowl. Strain the almonds from the oil and transfer them to a clean bowl. Reserve the oil and set it aside.

3. In a medium bowl, combine the orange zest, thyme, salt, and 2 tablespoons of the reserved oil. Add the olives and stir well to coat. Set the bowl aside.

FOR THE WHIPPED RICOTTA

1. In the bowl of a food processor, whip the ricotta, cream, and salt until smooth and creamy, 2 to 3 minutes. Stop the processor and scrape down the sides and bottom of the bowl as needed.

FOR THE TOAST

1. Preheat the oven to 500°F.

2. Arrange the bread on a large baking sheet. Lightly brush both sides of the bread with the oil.

3. Place in the oven and bake until golden brown, 1 to 2 minutes on each side. Keep an eye to avoid burning.

4. Remove the toasted bread from the oven, and cool on the pan for 5 minutes.

TO ASSEMBLE

1. Transfer the toast to a large plate or serving platter.

2. Stir the almonds into the olive mixture.

3. Spread the ricotta mixture on top of the toast, dividing it equally among the pieces. Top the ricotta with the olive-almond mixture.

4. Season with the salt and pepper. Lightly drizzle with the honey and the remaining reserved oil. Garnish with the sprigs of thyme. Serve at once.

ASHLEY'S TIP

Castelvetrano olives are a key ingredient that shouldn't be substituted. This type of olive is crunchy, buttery, and slightly sweet—and more importantly, its flavor won't overpower the other ingredients in this recipe. They're readily available in most chain grocery stores, but can also be ordered online.

Lemon-Rosemary Chicken Wings | SERVES 6 TO 8

Confession: I don't love deep-frying. But I do love chicken wings. So what's a girl to do? Bake and broil—that's what! I do this for all my chicken wing recipes, but it's an especially effective cooking method for these beauties. Coated in a lemony marinade that's spiked with fresh rosemary, balsamic vinegar, Dijon mustard, and honey, these wings are outrageously flavorful. The delightfully delicious glaze thickens and caramelizes as the wings bake, and they emerge from the oven juicy, fragrant, and just a little bit crispy at the edges. Sticky, sweet, and just slightly spicy . . . your guests will go wild over these! Serve with plenty of napkins.

CHICKEN WINGS

3½ pounds (1.6 kg) chicken wings, cut into sections

4 tablespoons (57 g) unsalted butter, melted

2 tablespoons (28 ml) olive oil

2½ teaspoons garlic powder

1 teaspoon salt

¾ teaspoon freshly ground black pepper

¼ teaspoon cayenne pepper

LEMON-ROSEMARY SAUCE

4 tablespoons (57 g) unsalted butter

1 shallot, finely diced

3 cloves garlic, minced

½ teaspoon red pepper flakes

¼ cup (85 ml) honey

3 tablespoons (42 ml) fresh lemon juice

1 tablespoon (14 ml) balsamic vinegar

1 tablespoon (10 g) fresh rosemary leaves, finely chopped

1 tablespoon (14 ml) country Dijon mustard

1 teaspoon water

1¼ teaspoons cornstarch

½ teaspoon fine sea salt

⅛ teaspoon freshly ground black pepper

8 sprigs fresh rosemary

1 large lemon, sliced into thin rounds

FOR THE WINGS

1. Preheat the oven to 400°F. Line a large, rimmed baking sheet with parchment paper and set it aside.
2. Dry the chicken wings thoroughly with paper towels, pressing down to remove as much excess moisture as possible. (The drier the wings, the crispier they'll bake up!)
3. Place the chicken wings in a large bowl and set the bowl aside.
4. In a small bowl, combine the melted butter, oil, garlic powder, salt, black pepper, and cayenne pepper. Pour this mixture over the wings and, using your hands, toss well to coat.
5. Spread the wings in a single layer on the prepared baking sheet, making sure none are touching. Bake until the wings are browned and crisp, about 50 minutes, using tongs to flip them over halfway through baking.

FOR THE SAUCE

1. In a small saucepan over medium heat, melt the butter. Add the shallot and cook, stirring occasionally, until softened, about 4 minutes.
2. Add the garlic and pepper flakes and cook for a minute, stirring constantly, or until fragrant. Then add the honey, lemon juice, vinegar, rosemary, and mustard. Bring the mixture to a slow boil, stirring constantly.
3. In a small bowl, whisk together the water and cornstarch to form a slurry, then pour this into the sauce and cook, stirring constantly, until it begins to thicken, about 45 seconds. Stir in the salt and black pepper, then remove the pan from the heat and set it aside.

TO ASSEMBLE

1. When the wings have finished baking, carefully remove the tray from the oven and set it aside. Increase the oven temperature to the broiler setting.
2. Transfer the wings to a large heatproof bowl. Pour the warm sauce over the wings and gently toss to coat.

continues on p. 46

3. Scatter the rosemary and lemon slices on the baking sheet, and gently toss with any remaining moisture on the sheet. Transfer the wings back to the prepared sheet, arranging them on top of the lemon slices and rosemary.

4. Place the pan on the middle rack in the oven and broil for 4 minutes, or until they're deeply golden brown but not burned. (Don't walk away—the broiler cooks quickly and the wings can burn in a matter of seconds.)

5. Carefully remove wings from the oven and serve warm right from the tray, or carefully transfer to a large serving platter. Serve with plenty of napkins!

Ultimate Meatball Sliders | YIELDS 24 SLIDERS

As a meatball fanatic, this is one of my all-time favorite recipes. But it's not just my favorite—it's probably the most popular recipe I serve at parties and get-togethers! And it's easy to see why: Homemade meatballs + tangy marinara sauce + cheesy buns = the ultimate comfort food! Loved equally by kids and adults, this is a crowd-pleasing recipe you can enjoy all year long. Just be sure to serve with plenty of napkins!

MARINARA SAUCE

2½ tablespoons (35 ml) olive oil

1 tablespoon (14 g) unsalted butter

5 cloves garlic, minced

¼ teaspoon red pepper flakes

1 (28-ounce/794-g) can crushed tomatoes with basil

1 teaspoon salt, more to taste

½ teaspoon granulated sugar

¼ cup (22 g) roughly chopped fresh basil leaves

1 teaspoon finely chopped fresh oregano leaves

MEATBALLS

1 pound (454 g) lean ground beef

1 pound (454 g) ground Italian sausage (sweet or spicy)

1 cup (99 g) finely grated Parmesan cheese

1 cup (50 g) panko breadcrumbs

¼ cup (40 g) finely grated yellow onion

2 teaspoons garlic powder

2 teaspoons onion powder

1½ teaspoons Italian seasoning

¾ teaspoon salt

½ teaspoon freshly ground black pepper

2 large eggs

½ cup (113 ml) lukewarm water

FOR THE SAUCE

1. In a large saucepan over medium heat, warm the oil and butter until shimmering. Add the garlic and pepper flakes and cook, stirring frequently, for 1 minute, or until garlic is fragrant—be sure not to let the garlic brown.

2. Add the tomatoes, salt, and sugar, and stir well to combine. Bring to a boil, then reduce the heat to medium-low and simmer, stirring frequently, for 25 minutes.

3. Add the basil and oregano and stir well to combine. Simmer for another 5 minutes, then taste and add more seasonings if needed.

4. Remove the pan from the heat, cover, and set it aside. (Note: Sauce can be made up to 48 hours in advance. Cool completely, then cover and refrigerate until needed. Rewarm before using.)

FOR THE MEATBALLS

1. Preheat the oven to 425°F. Line a large rimmed baking sheet with parchment paper and set it aside.

2. In a large bowl, combine the beef, sausage, Parmesan, breadcrumbs, grated onion, garlic powder, onion powder, Italian seasoning, salt, pepper, and eggs.

3. Slowly add the water, a few tablespoons at a time, mixing with your hands until everything is just combined. Don't overmix, or it will make the meatballs tough. The mixture should be very moist but still hold its shape when rolled into balls.

4. Using an ice cream scoop or large spoon, divide the meat mixture into 24 portions (about 2 tablespoons each), and roll each into a ball. Place the balls on the prepared baking sheet, leaving ½ inch between each ball.

5. Bake for 14 to 15 minutes, or until cooked through. Toss the meatballs into the marinara sauce and keep warm until ready to serve. (Note: Meatballs can be made up to 48 hours in advance. Cool completely and store in an airtight container, in the refrigerator until needed. Rewarm in the sauce before using.)

continues on p. 48

ITALIAN ASIAGO BUNS

24 small dinner rolls, sliced in half lengthwise

2 cups (227 g) coarsely shredded mozzarella cheese

2 tablespoons (28 ml) olive oil

¾ cup (75 g) finely shredded Asiago cheese

1½ tablespoons (21 g) Italian seasoning

FOR THE BUNS

1. (Note: Buns should be assembled and baked right before serving.) Preheat the oven to 375°F. Line a large baking sheet with parchment paper.
2. Place the bottom halves of the dinner rolls onto the baking sheet. Evenly sprinkle the rolls with the mozzarella.
3. Place the top halves of the dinner rolls onto the baking sheet, with the tops of the rolls facing up. Lightly brush with the oil, then sprinkle evenly with the Asiago and Italian seasoning.
4. Place the sheet in the oven and bake for 4 to 5 minutes, or until the mozzarella is melted and the tops of the buns are lightly golden brown.

TO ASSEMBLE

1. Top a bottom bun with a meatball and some extra sauce, then add the top bun. Repeat with all buns and meatballs. Serve warm.

Caramelized Onion Dip Snack Board | SERVES 6 TO 8

This just might be the prettiest veggie platter you've ever seen. All the colors and textures just make me so happy! No sad, pale celery sticks or dried-out baby carrots here. But I'm getting ahead of myself because the veggies are just part of this recipe. The real star of the show? Caramelized onion dip! And this is not your average (read: boring) dip. It's loaded with melt-in-your-mouth caramelized onions and flavored with fresh thyme, brown sugar, and a medley of spices and seasonings. In a word: fabulous! It's perfect for dipping crackers, veggies, chips, or anything else your little heart desires.

CARAMELIZED ONION DIP

- 3 tablespoons (42 g) unsalted butter
- 2 tablespoons (28 ml) olive oil, plus more for drizzling
- 3 pounds (1.36 kg) yellow onions, diced
- 1 tablespoon (14 g) packed light brown sugar
- 1½ teaspoons fresh thyme leaves, finely chopped
- 3 tablespoons (42 ml) water
- 1 tablespoon (14 ml) apple cider vinegar
- ½ teaspoon coarse Dijon mustard
- 8 ounces (227 g) full-fat cream cheese, room temperature
- 1 cup (227 g) full-fat sour cream, room temperature
- ⅓ cup (76 g) mayonnaise
- ½ teaspoon Worcestershire sauce
- ½ teaspoon Tabasco® sauce
- ½ teaspoon garlic powder
- ½ teaspoon onion powder
- ½ teaspoon fine sea salt
- ¼ teaspoon freshly ground black pepper
- Sprigs of fresh thyme, for garnish

FOR THE DIP

1. In a large skillet over medium-high heat, warm the butter and oil until shimmering. Add the onions, brown sugar, and thyme and cook, stirring occasionally, until the onions begin to brown, about 15 minutes. Stir in the water and, using a wooden spoon, scrape any browned bits from the bottom of the pan.
2. Reduce the heat to low and continue cooking, stirring occasionally, for 40 to 45 minutes, or until the onions are very soft and deep golden brown. (Note: If at any point the pan looks too dry, add another tablespoon of water.)
3. Carefully remove ¼ cup of the caramelized onions and set them aside to cool. Then cover and refrigerate until needed.
4. Stir the vinegar and mustard into the remaining onions and cook for 2 more minutes. Remove the pan from the heat and set it aside to cool.
5. In the bowl of a stand mixer fitted with the paddle attachment, or in a large bowl using a handheld electric mixer, combine the cream cheese, sour cream, mayonnaise, Worcestershire, Tabasco®, garlic powder, onion powder, salt, and pepper. Beat on medium speed until well combined.
6. Add the caramelized onions (except the ¼ cup reserved) and mix until combined.
7. Scrape the mixture into a serving bowl, cover, and chill for at least 30 minutes or up to 4 hours.
8. Right before serving, mix the dip again (it will separate a bit in the fridge), drizzle with a teaspoon of oil, and top with the reserved onions and thyme sprigs.

continues on p. 52

SNACK BOARD SUGGESTIONS

Broccoli florets

Broccolini stems

Bagel chips or pretzel crisps

Cucumbers, rounds or spears

Cauliflower florets (look for colorful varieties)

Cherry tomatoes

Celery sticks

Crackers

Crisp breadsticks

Endive leaves (a mix of green and red looks pretty)

Green beans, trimmed

Green olives

Marinated olives

Petite carrots (look for colorful heirloom varieties), cut lengthwise

Potato, pita, or tortilla chips

Radishes, trimmed and halved

Sugar snap peas

TO ASSEMBLE

1. Place the onion dip in the middle of a large serving board or platter.
2. Arrange the chips, crackers, and breadsticks in piles and stacks around the board.
3. Place the olives in a few small bowls and arrange them on the board. Then fill the rest of the board with piles of vegetables. Serve right away.

ASHLEY'S TIP

Seek out the freshest veggies available. Start by finding out what's in season, then head to your farmers' market, grocery store, or specialty shop and pick out the very best they have. We eat with our eyes first! Look for bright colors, firm textures, and check for a fresh scent. It's better to have a small selection of the best rather than a wide selection of mediocre options.

Garlic Parmesan Popcorn | SERVES 4 TO 6

Hosting a holiday movie night? Having the girls over for wine and afternoon gossip? Planning an epic game of Monopoly with the kids? This is the snack to make! Fresh garlic and rosemary give this popcorn plenty of flavor, and the addition of Parmesan cheese makes it borderline addicting. Popcorn is best eaten fresh, so pop your corn right before you plan on digging in!

- 2 tablespoons (28 ml) refined coconut oil or peanut oil
- ½ cup (105 g) popcorn kernels
- 4 tablespoons (57 g) unsalted butter
- 2 small cloves garlic, minced
- 1 tablespoon (10 g) finely chopped fresh rosemary leaves
- 1 tablespoon (14 ml) olive oil
- ½ cup (50 g) finely grated Parmesan cheese
- 1½ teaspoons garlic powder
- ½ teaspoon fine sea salt, plus more to taste
- ½ teaspoon freshly ground black pepper
- ½ teaspoon dried basil
- ¼ teaspoon cayenne pepper (optional)

1. In a large heavy pot over medium-high heat, warm the oil until shimmering. Add the popcorn and partially cover the pot with a lid. Once the popcorn kernels start to pop, reduce the heat to medium and cover the pot completely. Continue cooking, shaking the pot every 30 seconds, until the popping has reduced to a few seconds between each pop. Don't walk away, as the popcorn may burn.

2. Remove the pot from the heat and transfer the popcorn to a large bowl.

3. In a small saucepan over medium heat, melt the butter. Add the minced garlic and rosemary and cook, stirring constantly, for 1 minute, or just until fragrant (do not let the garlic burn).

4. Remove the pan from the heat and drizzle the butter mixture over the popcorn. Toss to coat. Drizzle the popcorn with the olive oil, then sprinkle with the Parmesan, garlic powder, salt, black pepper, basil, and cayenne pepper (if using). Toss again, ensuring the popcorn is evenly coated. Serve at once.

Prosciutto-Wrapped Jalapeño Poppers | YIELDS 20 POPPERS

If there are no poppers involved, is it even a party? (Joking, obviously!) But my love for these spicy little bites is very serious. Stuffed with not one, but FOUR kinds of cheese, and wrapped in thinly sliced prosciutto (so much better than bacon, if you ask me), these are simply irresistible!

1½ tablespoons (21 g) unsalted butter

1 large yellow onion (200 g), finely diced

2 teaspoons packed light brown sugar

2 teaspoons finely chopped fresh thyme leaves

2 teaspoons water

8 ounces (227 g) full-fat cream cheese, room temperature

½ cup (57 g) finely shredded fontina cheese

½ cup (57 g) finely shredded Asiago cheese

¼ cup (29 g) finely shredded sharp cheddar cheese

1 tablespoon (10 g) finely chopped fresh parsley

1 teaspoon garlic powder

¼ teaspoon onion powder

¼ teaspoon salt

⅛ teaspoon freshly ground black pepper

⅛ teaspoon cayenne pepper

½ cup (25 g) panko breadcrumbs

2 teaspoons olive oil

10 large, firm fresh jalapeño peppers (see Tips)

20 thin slices prosciutto

¼ cup (85 ml) good-quality honey (optional)

Sprigs of fresh thyme, for garnish (optional)

1. Preheat the oven to 350°F. Line a large baking sheet with parchment paper, then place an oven-safe wire rack on top. Set it aside.

2. In a medium sauté pan over medium heat, melt the butter. Add the onion and stir to coat. Add the brown sugar, thyme, and water. Cook, stirring occasionally, until the onions have softened and the water has evaporated, about 10 minutes.

3. Remove the onions from the heat and transfer to a large bowl. Add the cream cheese, fontina, Asiago, cheddar, parsley, garlic powder, onion powder, salt, black pepper, and cayenne pepper. Using a handheld electric mixer, beat the cream cheese mixture on medium-low speed until it's evenly combined, scraping down the sides and bottom of the bowl as needed. Set the mixture aside.

4. In a small bowl, combine the panko and oil, and mix well to combine. Set the bowl aside.

5. Wearing rubber gloves, cut the jalapeños in half lengthwise, taking care to cut them evenly. Remove the seeds and inner membranes, leaving the stem intact.

6. Divide the cheese filling equally among the jalapeño halves. Then sprinkle the panko evenly over the cheese, pressing it lightly so it sticks.

7. Wrap each stuffed jalapeño with a slice of prosciutto and stick a toothpick horizontally through the center to secure it in place.

8. Transfer the peppers to the prepared baking sheet, placing them on top of the wire rack. (Note: Make sure they're not tipping to one side or the filling will leak out during baking.)

9. Bake for 30 minutes, then increase the heat to 425°F and bake for 10 more minutes, or until the cheese is bubbling and prosciutto looks crispy.

10. Serve warm, drizzled with honey and garnished with sprigs of fresh thyme, if using.

ASHLEY'S TIP

Buy the largest, firmest jalapeños possible. They hold their shape well when baked and will hold more filling. Also look for jalapeños that are similar in size, which ensures they all finish baking at the same time.

Italian Hoagie Party Platter | YIELDS 6 HOAGIES (24 PIECES)

If you're not from Philadelphia (or South Jersey), you might be scratching your head and wondering, "What the heck is a hoagie?" It's essentially just a sandwich made on a very long roll. You may have seen them labeled as "submarine" or "hero" sandwiches. But in Philly, we call them hoagies, and they're kind of a big deal. They're sold everywhere from convenience stores to specialty shops. And Italian hoagies are, by far, the most well-known and popular variety. They're loaded with Italian meats, cheese, and plenty of crispy veggies. My recipe will help you not only make a killer hoagie, but assemble a professional-looking party platter your guests will love!

6 long Italian-style hoagie rolls

2½ tablespoons (35 ml) red wine vinegar

1 tablespoon (5 g) dried oregano

¼ cup (50 ml) olive oil

1½ pounds (681 g) thinly sliced prosciutto

1½ pounds (681 g) thinly sliced capicola

1½ pounds (681 g) thinly sliced genoa salami

1½ pounds (681 g) thinly sliced hot soppressata

1½ pounds (681 g) thinly sliced aged provolone cheese

5 large tomatoes, thinly sliced

3 cups shredded iceberg or romaine lettuce

1 large red onion, very thinly sliced

FOR SERVING

(Note: These items can typically be found in the condiments aisle at the grocery store or special ordered online)

Hot cherry peppers

Sweet pepper strips

Hot cherry pepper hoagie spread

Red wine vinegar

Olive oil

1. Slice the rolls lengthwise, cutting only halfway through.
2. In a small bowl, whisk together the vinegar and oregano. Slowly add the oil in a thin stream, whisking as you pour to emulsify the mixture. Drizzle a small amount of the vinegar mixture onto each roll. (Note: If you're preparing this recipe more than 30 minutes in advance, leave the rolls dry, and instead drizzle on top of each hoagie right before serving.)
3. Layer the rolls with the meats and cheese, adding ¼ pound of each deli meat and ¼ pound of cheese per roll. Top each roll with sliced tomatoes, lettuce, and onions. (Note: You can layer the meats, cheeses, and veggies however you find them most aesthetically pleasing.)
4. Slice each hoagie into four pieces. Pile the hoagie pieces onto a large serving platter.
5. Place the serving items into small bowls or dishes with serving spoons. Add the sides to the platter and serve at once!

ASHLEY'S TIP

The key to a good hoagie is great bread. If you can't find hoagie rolls at the grocery store, try your local Italian deli, sandwich shop, or bakery. You can also special-order hoagie rolls online that come from Philly! I'll often order a dozen or two from Goldbelly.com and store them in the freezer until needed.

Appetizers & Snacks

Brie Bites with Cranberry Chutney | YIELDS 24 BITES

Say hello to what I can easily declare is the prettiest appetizer in this book! Between the sparkling cranberries, thinly sliced brie, and fresh mint sprigs, these bites are a feast for the eyes! In our house, we call them cranberry Christmas bites, because they taste like all the flavors of Christmas wrapped up in one little bite. But they're perfect for any holiday party or festive event—not just Christmas!

SPARKLING CRANBERRIES

2 cups (396 g) granulated sugar, divided

1 cup (227 ml) water

2 cups (198 g) fresh or frozen cranberries (if frozen do not thaw)

CRANBERRY CHUTNEY

2 cups (198 g) fresh or frozen cranberries (if frozen do not thaw)

½ cup (113 ml) nonalcoholic ginger beer

½ cup (99 g) granulated sugar

¼ cup (53 g) packed brown sugar

2 tablespoons (39 ml) pure maple syrup

½ teaspoon ground cinnamon

¼ teaspoon ground ginger

⅛ teaspoon ground cloves

⅛ teaspoon ground allspice

⅛ teaspoon ground cardamom

1 large Granny Smith apple, peeled, cored, and finely diced

3 teaspoons finely grated orange zest

CROSTINI

1 French-style baguette, cut into 24 (½-inch) slices

⅓ cup (67 ml) olive oil

FOR SERVING

8 ounces (227 g) Brie cheese

1 medium Honeycrisp apple, cored and thinly sliced (optional)

Sprigs of fresh mint, for garnish (optional)

FOR THE CRANBERRIES

1. In a medium saucepan, combine 1 cup (198 g) of the sugar and the water and whisk well to combine.

2. Place the pan over medium heat and bring to a low simmer, whisking frequently, until the sugar has completely dissolved, 2 to 3 minutes.

3. Add the cranberries and, using a wooden spoon, stir to coat. Cook for 1 minute, then, using a slotted spoon, transfer the cranberries to a wire rack and dry for 10 minutes, or until still slightly sticky to the touch.

4. Add the remaining 1 cup (198 g) of sugar to a wide, shallow bowl. Add a few cranberries at a time, rolling them in the sugar until completely coated. Return the cranberries to the wire rack and set them aside to dry for at least 1 hour. (Note: Sparkling cranberries can be made up to 48 hours in advance. Store them in the refrigerator in an airtight container. If they lose any of their "sparkle", simply roll them in more sugar to freshen them up.)

FOR THE CHUTNEY

1. In a large saucepan, combine the cranberries, ginger beer, both sugars, maple syrup, and all the spices. Cook over medium heat, stirring occasionally, until the cranberries burst, 10 to 12 minutes.

2. Add the apple and orange zest and simmer, stirring occasionally, until the apples have softened and the mixture is very thick, about 8 minutes.

3. Transfer to a medium bowl and refrigerate until chilled. (Note: Chutney can be made up to 48 hours in advance. Store covered in the refrigerator until needed. Bring to room temperature for 30 minutes and stir well before using.)

FOR THE CROSTINI

1. Preheat the oven to 350°F. Lightly brush both sides of the baguette with the oil.

2. Arrange the slices in a single layer on a large rimmed baking sheet. Bake for 6 minutes, or until lightly golden brown, turning the crostini over once halfway through baking. Cool on the baking sheet for 5 minutes before using.

continues on p. 62

TO ASSEMBLE

1. Remove the Brie from the fridge 30 minutes before slicing. Cut into 24 thin slices.
2. Top a piece of crostini with a slice of Brie and an apple slice or two, if desired. Top with a tablespoon of the chutney. Press a few sparkling cranberries into the chutney.
3. Garnish with mint sprigs (if using) and place the crostini on a large serving platter. Serve at once.

Mini Crab Cakes with Spicy Remoulade | YIELDS 14 CRAB CAKES

Crab cakes will never go out of style! From dive bars to fine-dining establishments, you'll find them on almost any kind of restaurant's menu. And this is my tasty version: bite-size and fried to a crisp, these mini mouthfuls are packed with a pound of jumbo lump crabmeat and just enough seasoning to impart flavor without overwhelming the delicate crabmeat. I also include my recipe for spicy remoulade sauce, which is packed with flavor and should be served on the side. Toss a couple of lemon wedges on there, and you'll have an eye-catching platter perfect for any special occasion!

MINI CRAB CAKES

½ cup (113 ml) mayonnaise

1½ tablespoons (21 ml) fresh lemon juice

1½ teaspoons Old Bay® seasoning

1 teaspoon country Dijon mustard

1 teaspoon Worcestershire sauce

¼ teaspoon Tabasco® sauce

¼ teaspoon freshly ground black pepper

⅛ teaspoon sea salt

1 large egg yolk

1 pound (454 g) good-quality jumbo lump crabmeat, picked over for shells

1 cup (50 g) panko breadcrumbs, divided

¼ cup (50 ml) olive oil, plus more if needed

Lemon wedges, for serving

SPICY REMOULADE

¾ cup (170 ml) mayonnaise

3 tablespoons (28 g) finely diced celery

2 tablespoons (20 g) finely chopped fresh parsley

1½ tablespoons (21 ml) country Dijon mustard

1 tablespoon (14 ml) prepared horseradish

1 tablespoon (14 ml) ketchup

1 tablespoon (14 ml) fresh lemon juice

1½ teaspoons Worcestershire sauce

1 teaspoon Old Bay® seasoning

1 teaspoon Tabasco® sauce

1 clove garlic, minced

FOR THE CRAB CAKES

1. In a large glass measuring cup combine the mayonnaise, lemon juice, Old Bay®, mustard, Worcestershire, Tabasco®, pepper, salt, and egg yolk. Whisk well to combine.

2. In a large bowl, combine the mayonnaise mixture and the crabmeat, mixing gently with a rubber spatula just until combined. Carefully fold in ½ cup (25 g) of the panko, mixing until evenly combined.

3. Cover the bowl and refrigerate for at least 2 hours, and up to 12 hours.

4. When you're ready to cook, remove the crab mixture from the fridge. Place the remaining panko in a wide, shallow bowl and set it aside. Line a large plate with paper towels and set it aside.

5. Using a large cookie scoop, divide the crab mixture into 14 mounds (each about 3 tablespoons/50 g). Shape each mound into a firmly packed patty, about 1½ inches in diameter. Lightly coat the patties in the panko, covering both sides. Transfer the patties to a clean plate.

6. Cover the plate with plastic wrap and place it in the fridge for 10 minutes.

7. In the meantime, warm the oil in a medium skillet over medium heat until shimmering.

8. Carefully add the crab cakes to the oil, a few at a time, and cook for 3 minutes. Using a small fish spatula, carefully flip them over and continue cooking for 3 more minutes, or until golden brown. Transfer the cooked crab cakes to the paper towel-lined plate. Continue with the remaining crab cakes, adding more oil to the pan and adjusting the temperature, as needed.

9. Serve warm, with lemon wedges and spicy remoulade.

FOR THE SPICY REMOULADE

1. In a medium bowl, whisk together the remoulade ingredients until well combined.

2. Cover the bowl and refrigerate the remoulade for at least 2 hours. (Note: Remoulade can be made up to 12 hours in advance. Store covered, in the refrigerator, and mix well before serving.)

Four-Cheese Spinach Dip | SERVES 6 TO 8

Disclaimer: I don't really like spinach dip. But I love this spinach dip! I once ate half a pan right before going to a Pilates class and it was the best (and worst) decision of my life. Loaded with four varieties of cheese and topped with crunchy panko crumbs, this dip is pure perfection!

SPINACH DIP

Nonstick cooking spray

2 (10-ounce/283-g) bags frozen cut spinach

8 ounces (227 g) full-fat cream cheese

2 cups (227 g) shredded sharp white cheddar cheese

1 cup plus 2 tablespoons (139 g) shredded mozzarella cheese, divided

1 cup (99 g) finely shredded Parmesan cheese

¾ cup (170 ml) mayonnaise

¾ cup (170 g) sour cream

1 teaspoon Worcestershire sauce

1 teaspoon onion powder

1 teaspoon garlic powder

½ teaspoon freshly ground black pepper

½ teaspoon cayenne pepper

¼ teaspoon ground nutmeg

½ cup (25 g) panko breadcrumbs

CROSTINI

1 French-style baguette, cut into ½-inch diagonal slices

½ cup (100 ml) olive oil, plus more if needed

½ teaspoon garlic powder

¼ teaspoon sea salt

¼ teaspoon freshly ground black pepper

FOR THE DIP

1. Preheat the oven to 350°F. Lightly grease a 12-inch cast iron skillet or a 9 x 13-inch baking dish with nonstick cooking spray. Set it aside.

2. Place a fine-mesh strainer over a large bowl, leaving at least 2 inches of space between the bottom of the strainer and the bottom of the bowl. Line the strainer with three long layers of cheesecloth, then set it aside.

3. Place the spinach in a large saucepan and warm over medium heat, stirring frequently with a wooden spoon for 3 minutes, or until it's thawed and liquid has started to release. Remove the pan from the heat.

4. Place the spinach into the prepared strainer. Gather the edges of the cheesecloth, then twist and gently squeeze to force the liquid out. Continue until all the liquid has been removed. (Don't skimp on this step, or your spinach dip will be soggy.)

5. In a large bowl, combine the drained spinach, cream cheese, cheddar, 1 cup (113 g) of the mozzarella, the Parmesan, mayonnaise, sour cream, Worcestershire, onion powder, garlic powder, black pepper, cayenne pepper, and nutmeg. Mix with a rubber spatula until evenly combined.

6. Transfer the spinach mixture to the skillet or baking dish and smooth the top. (Note: Spinach dip can be made to this step, up to 24 hours in advance. Store, covered tightly, in the refrigerator. Remove from the refrigerator and uncover 30 minutes before baking. Then proceed with the steps below.)

7. Sprinkle evenly with the remaining 2 tablespoons (26 g) mozzarella and the panko.

8. Bake for 28 to 30 minutes, or until golden brown and bubbling. Serve at once, with crostini.

FOR THE CROSTINI

1. Preheat the oven to 375°F. In a small bowl, whisk together the oil, garlic powder, salt, and pepper. Lightly brush both sides of the baguette with the oil.

2. Arrange the slices in a single layer on a large rimmed baking sheet. Bake for 8 minutes, or until golden brown, turning the crostini over once halfway through baking. Cool completely on the baking sheet before using.

3
CHAPTER

Meals

Cooking for friends, family, and neighbors is my love language. It's a simple and extremely effective way to let people know just how much I care about them. I strongly believe there are a few things more special in life than sharing a meal with the people you love! So, in this chapter, I encourage you to do *just* that. Cook a meal, invite some great folks over, and enjoy every second of it. Whether you're looking to host a casual pasta night, a traditional holiday feast, or something in between, I hope your table will be surrounded by love and lots of smiling faces this season!

Holiday Hens with Wild Rice Pilaf | 70

Garlicky Shrimp Polenta | 73

Pan-Seared Cod in Lemon-Caper Sauce | 74

Meatball & Spinach Baked Ziti | 77

Lemon Risotto with Brown Butter Scallops | 79

Special Occasion Roast Beef with Roasted Carrots | 83

Chicken Parmesan for a Crowd | 84

Rigatoni Bolognese with Garlic Bread | 87

Herb-Crusted Salmon with Mashed Potatoes | 90

Holiday Hens with Wild Rice Pilaf | SERVES 4 TO 8

Looking for a showstopping holiday dinner party recipe? This is it! Cornish game hens are so elegant and always impress. Covered in a cranberry-orange glaze and roasted until golden brown, these hens are served with a stunning wild rice pilaf sure to please!

CRANBERRY ORANGE-GLAZED HENS

4 Cornish game hens (about 2 pounds/908 g each)

3 tablespoons (42 g) unsalted butter

1 shallot, minced

1 cup (227 ml) fresh orange juice

1 cup (100 g) cranberries, fresh or frozen, if frozen, do not thaw

¼ cup (53 g) packed light brown sugar

2 tablespoons (24 g) finely grated orange zest

2 tablespoons (35 ml) pure maple syrup

2 sprigs fresh rosemary

½ teaspoon chili powder

½ cup (170 g) orange marmalade

1½ teaspoons balsamic vinegar

Salt and freshly ground black pepper to taste

WILD RICE PILAF

1½ cups (340 g) royal blend rice

2¼ cups (511 ml) chicken stock

½ teaspoon salt

1 tablespoon (14 ml) olive oil

5 ounces (142 g) pancetta, diced

4 tablespoons (57 g) unsalted butter

3 stalks celery, diced

2 medium yellow onions, diced

3 cloves garlic, minced

2 teaspoons fresh thyme leaves, finely chopped

1 teaspoon fresh rosemary leaves, finely chopped

¼ teaspoon salt

¼ teaspoon freshly ground black pepper

½ cup (57 g) chopped salted pistachios

½ cup (85 g) dried cranberries

FOR THE HENS

1. Preheat the oven to 400°F. Pat the hens dry with several layers of paper towels—get as much moisture off them as possible. Set hens aside.

2. In a medium saucepan over medium heat, melt the butter. Add the shallot and sauté for about 6 minutes, stirring occasionally, until translucent.

3. Add the orange juice, cranberries, brown sugar, orange zest, maple syrup, rosemary, and chili powder. Bring to a boil, then reduce the heat to a simmer. Cook for 10 to 15 minutes, mashing the cranberries as they start to burst, or until thickened. Remove the pan from the heat and discard the rosemary sprigs. Stir in the marmalade and balsamic. Set aside to cool.

4. Season the hens liberally with salt and pepper. Using a basting brush, paint each hen generously with the cranberry-orange glaze. Cover the wing tips with small pieces of aluminum foil to prevent burning.

5. Place the glazed hens in a large, enameled cast iron Dutch oven or in a large roasting pan and roast for 20 minutes. Remove the hens from the oven and carefully reglaze them. Continue roasting for 20 more minutes.

6. Reglaze once more. Return the hens to the oven and roast for 25 more minutes, or until the thighs register 165°F and the breasts register 170°F on an instant-read thermometer. If the hens are getting too brown, loosely tent the pan with a piece of aluminum foil and continue roasting. (Note: This is a good time to start making the pilaf.)

7. Remove the hens from the oven and rest for 10 minutes in the pan. Serve warm, over the rice pilaf.

FOR THE PILAF

1. Place the rice in a fine-mesh strainer and rinse it under cold running water, swishing it around until the water runs clear. Set the rice aside.

2. In a medium saucepan bring the chicken stock to a boil over high heat. Add the salt, then stir in the rinsed rice. Cover with a lid and reduce the heat to low. Simmer for 15 minutes. Then remove the rice from the heat and let it stand, covered, for 5 more minutes.

3. In the meantime, warm the oil in a large skillet over medium heat. Add the pancetta and cook, stirring frequently, until crispy.

4. Add the butter and cook until melted. Stir in the celery and onions and cook, stirring frequently, until the vegetables have softened, 6 to 8 minutes. Add the garlic, thyme, rosemary, salt, and pepper and cook for 5 more minutes.

5. Add in the cooked rice and stir well to combine. Stir in the pistachios and cranberries. Serve warm.

Garlicky Shrimp Polenta | SERVES 4 TO 6

My friend Michelle first introduced me to polenta. Her family actually threw polenta parties! I can't remember all the details or all the creative ways they served polenta, but I do remember it being a very delicious event! This memory inspired me to create my own trademark polenta dish. Featuring cheesy polenta, juicy shrimp, peppers, and onions, you could say this is my Italian-inspired version of shrimp and grits! Total Comfort food!

POLENTA

4 cups (907 ml) chicken bone broth, plus more if needed

2 cups (454 ml) whole milk

1½ cups (234 g) coarse polenta

½ cup (57 g) finely grated Parmesan cheese

½ cup (57 g) finely grated Asiago cheese

2½ tablespoons (35 g) unsalted butter

½ teaspoon salt, plus more to taste

¼ teaspoon freshly ground black pepper, plus more to taste

GARLICKY SHRIMP

3 tablespoons (42 ml) olive oil, divided

1½ pounds (681 g) large shrimp, peeled, deveined, and patted dry

1 teaspoon salt, divided, plus more to taste

½ teaspoon freshly ground black pepper, divided, plus more to taste

2 medium red bell peppers, diced

2 medium green bell peppers, diced

1 large red onion, diced

8 cloves garlic, minced

¼ teaspoon red pepper flakes, plus more to taste

¼ cup (57 g) tomato paste

½ cup (113 ml) dry white wine

½ cup (113 ml) chicken bone broth

3 tablespoons (42 ml) heavy cream

3 tablespoons (30 g) finely chopped fresh basil

2 tablespoons (20 g) finely chopped fresh parsley, plus more for garnish

¼ cup (43 grams) thinly sliced scallions, green part only, for garnish

FOR THE POLENTA

1. In a large saucepan over medium-high heat combine the broth and milk and bring to a rolling boil.

2. Slowly add the polenta, whisking constantly. Reduce the heat to medium-low and continue cooking for 45 to 50 minutes, whisking frequently, until the polenta is soft, thick, and creamy. If the polenta mixture thickens too quickly before it's fully cooked, simply add a little more broth or water, and continue cooking. (Note: You'll want to start cooking the shrimp when you have about 20 minutes left on the polenta, so they're ready to be served at the same time.)

3. Remove the polenta from the heat and whisk in the Parmesan, Asiago, butter, salt, and pepper, mixing until the butter and cheeses have completely melted. Taste the polenta and add salt and pepper as needed.

FOR THE SHRIMP

1. In a large skillet over medium-high heat warm 1½ tablespoons (21 ml) of the oil until shimmering. While the pan heats up, gently pat the shrimp dry with paper towels, pressing out any excess moisture. Season the shrimp with a ½ teaspoon of the salt and a ¼ teaspoon of the black pepper.

2. Add the shrimp to the pan and cook for 2 minutes per side, or until light pink all over. (Shrimp cooks very quickly, so don't walk away.) Transfer the shrimp to a clean plate and set it aside.

3. Add the remaining 1½ tablespoons (21 ml) of the oil to the skillet, then add the bell peppers and onion, and cook 6 minutes, stirring occasionally, until the vegetables have slightly softened.

4. Stir in the garlic, pepper flakes, and remaining salt and pepper and cook, stirring frequently, for 1 minute, or until fragrant. Do not let the garlic brown.

5. Add the tomato paste and wine and, using a wooden spoon, mix thoroughly, breaking up the tomato paste until a smooth sauce has formed. Add the broth and cook for 5 minutes, stirring occasionally.

6. Stir in the shrimp. Reduce the heat to low and slowly stir in the cream. Then add the basil and parsley and cook, stirring frequently, for 2 more minutes.

7. Remove the pan from the heat. Taste and season with salt and black pepper as needed. (Note: You can set the pan aside and cover tightly with foil for a few minutes if you need to keep warm while you finish the polenta.)

8. Spoon the polenta into bowls or onto a large platter, and top with the garlicky shrimp and peppers. Garnish with chopped parsley and scallions and serve at once.

Pan-Seared Cod in Lemon-Caper Sauce | SERVES 4 TO 6

Of all the recipes I've posted on my website, I never thought it would be a cod recipe that went viral. And yet, that's exactly what happened a few years ago when I shared my recipe for pan-seared cod. Which leads me to believe you guys really love cod. And I don't blame you: It's delicious, not too fishy, and is a blank canvas just begging to be livened up with flavor. So, when I was developing this recipe, I chose bold, bright flavors like lemon, brown butter, and white wine. The result? Absolute perfection!

ORZO

½ teaspoon salt

12 ounces (340 g) orzo pasta

3 tablespoons (42 ml) olive oil

LEMON-CAPER SAUCE

2 sticks (227 g) unsalted butter

10 cloves garlic, thinly sliced

1 tablespoon (12 g) finely grated lemon zest

1 teaspoon salt, more to taste

½ teaspoon freshly ground black pepper, more to taste

½ teaspoon red pepper flakes, more to taste

1 cup (227 ml) white wine

1½ teaspoons granulated sugar

½ cup (92 g) drained capers, rinsed

⅓ cup (76 ml) fresh lemon juice, more to taste

2 tablespoons (20 g) chopped fresh parsley

PAN-SEARED COD

2 pounds (908 g) fresh cod, cut into 6 fillets

Salt and freshly ground black pepper, to taste

2 tablespoons (28 ml) olive oil

2 tablespoons (28 g) unsalted butter

1½ tablespoons (15 g) chopped fresh parsley, for garnish

Lemon slices, for garnish

FOR THE ORZO

1. Bring a large pot of water to a rolling boil. Add the salt, then add the pasta and cook for 6 minutes, or until al dente. (Note: This is a good time to get started on the sauce.)

2. Drain the pasta well and transfer to a medium bowl. Toss with the oil, mixing well to evenly coat. Cover the bowl tightly with foil and set it aside until needed.

FOR THE SAUCE

1. In a large skillet over medium heat, melt the butter. Continue cooking, swirling the pan occasionally, until the butter turns a golden-brown color, about 6 to 7 minutes.

2. Add the garlic, lemon zest, salt, black pepper, and pepper flakes and cook for 1 to 2 minutes, or until the garlic is fragrant.

3. Add the wine and sugar and reduce the heat to medium. Simmer for 5 minutes, then toss in the capers and cook for 2 more minutes. (Note: You can keep the sauce warm at this stage by reducing the heat to low and stirring occasionally, for up to 5 minutes.)

4. Remove the skillet from the heat and stir in the lemon juice and parsley. Taste and add more seasonings, as needed.

FOR THE COD

1. Gently pat the cod fillets dry with paper towels, pressing out any excess moisture. Season both sides of the fillets with salt and pepper. Set fillets aside.

2. In a large cast iron skillet over medium heat, warm the oil until shimmering. Then add the butter and heat until completely melted.

3. Add the fillets to the skillet and cook until golden brown on the underside, about 4 minutes. Using a long fish spatula, carefully flip the fillets over and continue cooking for 3 more minutes, or until cooked through. Don't overcook or it will fall apart and dry out.

TO ASSEMBLE

1. Pour half of the lemon-caper sauce over the orzo. Toss well to combine. Transfer the orzo to a large serving platter.

2. Top the orzo with the fillets, then spoon the remaining lemon-caper sauce over the fillets. Sprinkle with parsley and add lemon slices for garnish. Serve at once.

Meatball & Spinach Baked Ziti | SERVES 6 TO 8

A big pan of good old baked ziti—it just can't be beat! Especially if you're looking to please a crowd. My spin on the classic? Mini meatballs . . . mini sausage meatballs, to be exact! They make this dish extra hearty and delicious. My second twist? I snuck some greens into the sauce by adding basil, parsley, oregano, and spinach! So refreshing! I love serving this with Caesar salad (page 111) and plenty of wine!

SAUSAGE MEATBALLS

1 pound (454 g) sweet Italian sausage, casings removed

¾ cup (38 g) panko breadcrumbs

½ cup (50 g) finely grated Parmesan cheese

1 large egg

1 clove garlic, minced

½ cup (113 ml) lukewarm water

MARINARA SAUCE

¼ cup (50 ml) olive oil

1 large onion, finely diced

8 cloves garlic, minced

¼ teaspoon red pepper flakes

3 tablespoons (42 g) tomato paste

⅔ cup (151 ml) dry red wine

2 (28-ounce/794-g) cans crushed tomatoes with basil

1 teaspoon Italian seasoning

1 teaspoon salt, plus more to taste

½ teaspoon freshly ground black pepper, plus more to taste

5 ounces (142 g) baby spinach

½ cup (45 g) chopped fresh basil leaves

2 tablespoons (20 g) chopped fresh parsley

2 teaspoons finely chopped fresh oregano leaves

1½ teaspoons granulated sugar

FOR THE MEATBALLS

1. Preheat the oven to 400°F. Line a large baking sheet with parchment paper and set it aside.

2. In a large bowl combine the sausage, panko, Parmesan, egg, and garlic.

3. Slowly add the water, a few tablespoons at a time, mixing with your hands until everything is just combined. (Don't overmix or the meatballs will be tough.) The mixture should be very moist but still hold its shape when rolled into balls.

4. Using a small spring-loaded measuring scoop or spoon, scoop about 2 teaspoons of the sausage mixture and roll it into a ball. Place the ball on the prepared baking sheet. Repeat with the remaining sausage mixture.

5. Bake for 12 minutes, or until cooked through. Remove the pan from the oven and set it aside. (Note: Meatballs can be made up to 48 hours in advance. Cool completely and store in an airtight container, in the refrigerator, until needed.)

FOR THE SAUCE

1. In a large saucepan over medium heat warm the oil until shimmering. Add the onion and cook for 5 minutes, stirring frequently, until soft and translucent.

2. Add the garlic and pepper flakes and cook for another minute, or until fragrant. Don't let the garlic brown.

3. Stir in the tomato paste. Then add the wine and stir to combine. Cook for 5 minutes.

4. Add the tomatoes, Italian seasoning, salt, and black pepper, and stir well to combine. Bring the sauce to a boil, then reduce the heat to medium-low and simmer for 45 minutes, stirring occasionally.

5. Stir in the spinach, basil, parsley, oregano, and sugar and cook for 5 more minutes. Taste the sauce and add salt and pepper as needed.

6. Remove the sauce from the heat and allow to cool slightly before using it in the baked ziti. (Note: Sauce can be made up to 48 hours in advance. Cool completely, then cover and refrigerate until needed.)

continues on p. 78

RICOTTA MIXTURE

15 ounces (425 g) whole-milk ricotta cheese

5 ounces (141 g) fontina cheese, shredded

½ cup (50 g) finely grated Parmesan cheese

2 tablespoons (20 g) finely chopped fresh parsley

2 tablespoons (20 g) finely chopped fresh basil

1 large egg plus 1 egg yolk

⅛ teaspoon salt

⅛ teaspoon freshly ground black pepper

BAKED ZITI

Nonstick cooking spray

½ teaspoon salt

1 pound (454 g) ziti or penne pasta

4 ounces (113 g) low-moisture mozzarella cheese, finely shredded

5 ounces (141 g) fontina cheese, cut into ¼-inch cubes

1 tablespoon (10 g) chopped fresh parsley

FOR THE RICOTTA MIXTURE

1. In a large bowl, combine all the ingredients. Stir together until just smooth. Set it aside.

TO ASSEMBLE AND BAKE

1. Preheat the oven to 375°F. Grease a 9 x 13-inch baking dish (at least 4.5-quart capacity) with nonstick cooking spray and set it aside.

2. Bring a large pot of water to a rolling boil. Add the salt, then add the pasta and cook for exactly 4 minutes. The pasta will still be very hard. Drain the pasta well.

3. Pour the pasta into a large bowl, then stir in 1½ cups (340 g) of the marinara sauce and half of the meatballs.

4. Spread 1 cup (227 g) of the remaining marinara sauce onto the bottom of the prepared baking dish. Then spoon half of the ricotta mixture on top, dropping it in random dots over the sauce.

5. Pour the pasta on top of this mixture. Then evenly dot with the remaining ricotta.

6. Pour the remaining sauce over the ricotta, then top with the remaining meatballs.

7. Evenly sprinkle the mozzarella on top, then dot with the fontina.

8. Bake for 30 minutes or until the cheese is melted and bubbling. If you want extra crispy, golden cheese, turn on the broiler for about 30 seconds before removing the baked ziti from the oven. (Don't walk away, as it can burn quickly!)

9. Garnish with a sprinkle of fresh parsley and serve warm.

Lemon Risotto with Brown Butter Scallops | SERVES 4

This is definitely a special-occasion meal, perfect for those nights you really want to impress! The combination of creamy risotto and juicy scallops is irresistible and a total treat. Good-quality scallops are on the pricier side, so I like to make this recipe for more intimate dinner parties. Serve with dry white wine or a few bottles of bubbly!

LEMON RISOTTO

4 cups (907 ml) vegetable stock

2 cups (454 ml) chicken bone broth

3 tablespoons (42 ml) olive oil, divided

2 tablespoons (28 g) unsalted butter

½ teaspoon red pepper flakes

3 shallots, finely diced

1 stalk celery, finely diced

1 large clove garlic, minced

1 teaspoon salt, plus more to taste

¼ teaspoon freshly ground black pepper, plus more to taste

1 cup (227 g) arborio rice

½ cup (113 ml) dry white wine

1 cup (100 g) Parmesan cheese, finely grated

2 tablespoons (20 g) finely chopped fresh dill, plus more for garnish

2 tablespoons (20 g) finely chopped fresh parsley, plus more for garnish

2 tablespoons (20 g) finely chopped fresh chives, plus more for garnish

2½ tablespoons (35 ml) fresh lemon juice

1 teaspoon finely grated lemon zest, plus more for garnish

BROWN BUTTER SAUCE

4 tablespoons (57 g) unsalted butter

3 cloves garlic, minced

½ teaspoon salt

¼ teaspoon freshly ground black pepper

¼ teaspoon red pepper flakes

1 teaspoon finely grated lemon zest

⅓ cup (76 ml) dry white wine (I like Sauvignon Blanc)

2 tablespoons (28 ml) lemon juice

FOR THE RISOTTO

1. In a large saucepan, combine the stock and broth and bring to a simmer over medium heat.

2. In the meantime, in a separate large saucepan over medium heat, warm 1 tablespoon (14 ml) of the oil and the butter until shimmering. Add the pepper flakes, shallots, and celery, and cook for 6 minutes, stirring frequently, until the celery is tender and the shallots have softened. Add the garlic, salt, and pepper, and cook for 1 more minute, or until fragrant.

3. Add the rice and cook 3 to 4 minutes, stirring frequently, until lightly toasted. Add the wine and cook about 3 minutes, stirring occasionally, until absorbed.

4. Add 1 cup of the warm stock mixture to the rice and cook, stirring constantly, until absorbed. Repeat, adding more stock, 1 cup at a time, until the rice is al dente but creamy in texture, about 20 minutes. (Note: This is a good time to start making the sauce.)

5. Remove the risotto from the heat and stir in the Parmesan, dill, parsley, chives, lemon juice, and lemon zest. Taste and season with salt and black pepper, as needed. Then stir in the remaining 2 tablespoons (28 ml) of oil.

FOR THE SAUCE

1. In a large skillet over medium heat, melt the butter. Continue cooking, swirling the pan occasionally, until the butter turns a golden-brown color, about 5 minutes.

2. Add the garlic, salt, black pepper, pepper flakes, and lemon zest and cook for 1 minute, or until the garlic is fragrant. Add the wine and reduce the heat to medium-low. Simmer the sauce for 5 minutes. (Note: This is a good time to start searing the scallops. You can keep the sauce warm at this stage by reducing the heat to low and stirring occasionally, for up to an additional 5 minutes, if needed.)

3. Stir in the lemon juice, parsley, and dill, and mix well to combine. Remove from heat and serve with scallops, as directed below.

continues on p. 80

1 tablespoon (10 g) finely chopped fresh parsley

1 tablespoon (10 g) finely chopped fresh dill

SCALLOPS

1 pound (454 g) sea scallops

1 tablespoon (14 g) unsalted butter

2 teaspoons olive oil

Salt and freshly ground black pepper

FOR THE SCALLOPS

1. Remove the tiny side muscle from the scallops (if they have one), then rinse them with cold water. Gently pat the scallops dry with paper towels, pressing out any excess moisture. Set them aside on a paper towel-lined plate.

2. In a large sauté pan over medium-high heat, warm the butter and oil until shimmering.

3. While the pan heats up, generously season the scallops with salt and pepper.

4. Working in batches, add the scallops to the pan in a single layer, making sure they are not touching. Sear the scallops for about 90 seconds, then gently flip them over and cook for 1 to 2 more minutes, or until both sides are golden brown. Remove the pan from the heat.

5. Add the seared scallops to the brown butter sauce and, using a spoon, drizzle the warm sauce all over them. Divide the risotto among shallow bowls. Top each bowl with a few scallops and brown butter sauce. Garnish with fresh dill, parsley, chives, lemon zest, and freshly ground black pepper, if desired.

Special Occasion Roast Beef with Roasted Carrots | SERVES 4 TO 6

Everyone always gets excited when I make this roast. And I get it—there's just something about a giant roast that makes an occasion feel extra special. And bonus points because it smells absolutely intoxicating as it cooks in the oven. I like to serve this with tender roasted carrots, mashed potatoes, and plenty of wine.

ROAST BEEF

- 6 pounds (2.72 kg) boneless ribeye roast
- 1 tablespoon (14 g) kosher salt
- 2½ teaspoons freshly ground black pepper
- 2 tablespoons (28 ml) olive oil, divided
- ½ cup (113 g) Dijon mustard
- ⅓ cup (114 g) prepared horseradish
- 8 cloves garlic, minced
- ¼ cup (40 g) finely chopped fresh parsley
- 2 tablespoons (20 g) finely chopped fresh thyme leaves
- 1 tablespoon (10 g) finely chopped fresh rosemary leaves

ROASTED CARROTS

- 10 large carrots, cut into ½ x 3-inch pieces (I like orange, purple, and yellow heirloom carrots, but plain carrots work fine, too)
- 3 tablespoons (42 ml) olive oil
- 2 tablespoons (42 ml) honey
- 1 teaspoon salt
- ½ teaspoon freshly ground black pepper
- 1 large red onion, halved vertically and cut into ½-inch pieces
- 1½ tablespoons (15 g) finely chopped fresh rosemary leaves
- 1 tablespoon (14 ml) fresh lemon juice
- 1½ tablespoons (15 g) chopped fresh parsley

FOR THE ROAST BEEF

1. Place an oven rack in the lower third of the oven. Preheat the oven to 450°F.
2. Season the roast with the salt and pepper. Set it aside.
3. In a large cast-iron skillet over medium-high heat, warm 1 tablespoon (14 ml) of the oil until it shimmers. Add the roast and cook until browned on both sides, about 3 minutes per side.
4. Remove the pan from the heat and transfer the roast to a roasting pan. Roast for 20 minutes.
5. In the meantime, in a medium bowl, combine the remaining 1 tablespoon (14 ml) of oil, the mustard, horseradish, garlic, parsley, thyme, and rosemary, mixing until a paste is formed. Set it aside.
6. When the 20 minutes are up, carefully remove the pan from the oven and reduce the temperature to 350°F.
7. Using a pastry brush, generously coat the tops and sides of the roast with the herbed mustard sauce. Return the pan to the oven and continue cooking for 1 hour and 15 minutes (rotating the pan every 30 minutes for even browning), or until the internal temperature reaches 120°F on a meat thermometer.
8. Remove the pan from the oven and cover tightly with aluminum foil. Let the meat rest for at least 30 minutes before slicing.
9. When ready to serve, cut the roast into ½-inch slices and transfer to a large serving platter.

FOR THE CARROTS

1. Preheat the oven to 425°F. Line a large baking sheet with parchment paper and set it aside.
2. In a large bowl, combine the carrots, oil, honey, salt, and pepper. Spread in a single layer on the prepared baking sheet and bake for 25 minutes, flipping the carrots and rotating the baking sheet at the halfway point.
3. Carefully remove the pan from the oven and add the onion and rosemary. Toss well to coat. Reduce the temperature to 400°F, then return the pan to the oven and continue roasting for 20 more minutes, or until the carrots and onions are tender.
4. Remove the pan from the oven and transfer the carrots to a large serving platter. Drizzle with the lemon juice and sprinkle with the parsley. Serve warm, with the roast beef.

Chicken Parmesan for a Crowd | SERVES 8

If you're looking to feed a large crowd and prefer to cook just one recipe, make it this one! Because this chicken parmesan is so much more than just chicken: It includes pasta, homemade sauce, tender chicken cutlets covered in cheese, and even a simple salad that can be served right on top. You'll want to bust out your biggest serving platter(s) for this recipe because it really does serve an army.

MARINARA SAUCE

⅔ cup (133 ml) olive oil

1 large onion, finely chopped

8 cloves garlic, minced

½ teaspoon red pepper flakes

½ cup (113 ml) dry red wine

2 tablespoons (28 g) tomato paste

2 (28-ounce/794-g) cans crushed tomatoes with basil

1 teaspoon granulated sugar

2 teaspoons salt, plus more to taste

½ teaspoon freshly ground black pepper

½ cup (45 g) roughly chopped fresh basil leaves

2 tablespoons (20 g) roughly chopped fresh parsley

1 tablespoon (10 g) roughly chopped fresh oregano leaves

CHICKEN

4 boneless, skinless chicken breasts (2.25 pounds/1.13 kg total)

2 cups (240 g) all-purpose flour

¾ teaspoon salt

½ teaspoon freshly ground black pepper

3 large eggs

1 tablespoon (14 ml) water

2 cups (100 g) panko breadcrumbs

½ cup (50 g) finely grated Parmesan cheese

1 teaspoon garlic powder

1 teaspoon Italian seasoning

⅓ cup (67 ml) olive oil

8 ounces (226 g) fontina cheese, shredded

12 ounces (340 g) low-moisture mozzarella cheese, thinly sliced

FOR THE SAUCE

1. In a large saucepan over medium heat, warm the oil until shimmering. Add the onion and cook for 5 minutes, stirring frequently, until soft and translucent.

2. Add the garlic and pepper flakes and cook for another minute, or until fragrant. Don't let the garlic brown.

3. Stir in the wine and allow the mixture to simmer for a minute. As it simmers, use a wooden spoon to scrape the bottom of the pan and mix well. Stir in the tomato paste.

4. Add the tomatoes and stir well to combine. Increase the heat to medium-high and bring the sauce to a boil. Then reduce the heat to a simmer, and cook the sauce for 30 minutes, stirring frequently.

5. Stir in the sugar, salt, black pepper, basil, parsley, and oregano and cook for 15 more minutes. Taste and add more seasonings, as needed.

6. Keep the sauce warm, on the lowest heat setting, stirring occasionally. (Note: Sauce can be made up to 48 hours in advance. Cool completely, then cover and refrigerate until needed. Rewarm before using.)

FOR THE CHICKEN

1. Preheat the oven to 425°F. Line a large baking sheet with parchment paper and place a large oven-safe wire rack on top. Set it aside.

2. Using a large chef's knife, carefully cut the chicken breasts in half, crosswise. You should end up with eight ¼-inch-thick chicken cutlets. (If they are thicker, place the cutlet between two pieces of wax paper and use a mallet to gently pound to ¼-inch thickness.) Set the chicken aside.

3. In a large shallow bowl, combine the flour, salt, and pepper. Set it aside.

4. In a separate large shallow bowl, beat the eggs and water until well combined. Set the bowl aside.

5. In a third large shallow bowl, combine the breadcrumbs, Parmesan, garlic powder, and Italian seasoning.

6. Working with one cutlet at a time, dredge in the flour mixture, shaking off any excess flour before transferring to a large plate.

7. Dip each cutlet in the egg mixture, then dredge each side in the breadcrumb mixture, pressing the coating firmly onto the chicken so it sticks.

continues on p. 86

ARUGULA SALAD

2 cups (71 g) baby arugula

2 tablespoons (28 ml) olive oil

1 tablespoon (14 ml) balsamic vinegar

½ teaspoon salt

¼ teaspoon freshly ground black pepper

¼ cup (29 g) freshly shaved Parmesan cheese, plus more for serving

PASTA

½ teaspoon salt

1 pound (454 g) spaghetti, or your favorite pasta

8. Place all the breaded cutlets onto a large plate and set them aside.
9. In a large cast-iron skillet over medium heat, warm the oil until shimmering. Fry the cutlets, two at a time, until golden brown, 2½ minutes per side. Repeat with all cutlets, adding more oil to the skillet and adjusting the heat as needed.
10. Transfer the chicken cutlets to the prepared baking sheet, placing them on top of the wire rack.

FOR THE SALAD

1. In a large bowl, toss together the arugula, oil, vinegar, salt, pepper, and Parmesan. Set the bowl aside. (Note: Salad should be made right before serving for best results.)

FOR THE PASTA

1. Bring a large pot of water to a rolling boil over high heat. Add the salt, then stir in the pasta. Cook for 8 minutes, or until al dente.
2. Drain the pasta well. Keep the pasta in the strainer and set it aside.

TO ASSEMBLE

1. Spoon 2 cups of the marinara sauce over the cutlets, spreading about ¼ cup of sauce on each cutlet. Evenly sprinkle the chicken cutlets with the fontina. Then top with the mozzarella. Place the baking sheet in the oven and bake until the cheese is melted and bubbling, about 6 to 7 minutes. (Note: This is a good time to make the arugula salad; see instructions above.)
2. Toss the cooked pasta in the remaining marinara sauce, mixing well to evenly coat the noodles. Transfer the pasta to a very large serving platter. (You can also use a baking sheet or baking dish.)
3. Remove the chicken from the oven and place the chicken cutlets on top of the pasta. Top with the arugula salad (or serve it on the side) and additional shaved Parmesan, if desired. Serve at once.

Rigatoni Bolognese with Garlic Bread | SERVES 6 TO 8

This is a meal I often dream about! Perfectly cooked rigatoni smothered in a hearty Bolognese sauce, served with crispy garlic bread on the side. It's nothing super fancy, but it is super special. This recipe doesn't really need anything more, but a simple arugula salad on the side and a good bottle of wine wouldn't hurt!

RIGATONI BOLOGNESE

2 tablespoons (28 ml) olive oil

5 ounces (142 g) pancetta, diced

1 pound (454 g) sweet Italian sausage, casings removed

1 pound (454 g) ground beef

2 small carrots, diced

1 large yellow onion, finely chopped

1 stalk celery, finely chopped

10 cloves garlic, minced

½ teaspoon red pepper flakes

3 tablespoons (42 g) tomato paste

1 cup (227 ml) dry red Italian wine

½ cup (113 ml) beef stock

2 (28-ounce/794-g) cans crushed tomatoes with basil

¾ teaspoon salt, more to taste

¼ teaspoon freshly ground black pepper, more to taste

¼ cup (57 ml) water

½ cup (45 g) chopped fresh basil

3 tablespoons (30 g) chopped fresh parsley

1 tablespoon (10 g) chopped fresh oregano

½ teaspoon granulated sugar

1 pound (454 g) rigatoni pasta

FOR THE RIGATONI

1. In a large saucepan heat the oil over medium heat. Add the pancetta and cook, stirring occasionally, for 5 to 6 minutes, or until it is browned.

2. Add the sausage and beef and, using a wooden spoon, break the meat up into small pieces. Continue cooking for 5 to 6 minutes, stirring occasionally, until the meat is browned and no pink remains.

3. Add the carrots, onion, and celery and continue cooking, stirring occasionally, for 6 to 8 minutes, or until the vegetables have softened and the onions are almost translucent.

4. Add the garlic and pepper flakes and cook for 1 minute, or until fragrant.

5. Stir in the tomato paste and cook for 30 seconds. Then add the wine and stir to combine. Cook for 5 minutes. Then stir in the beef stock, tomatoes, salt, and pepper and stir well to combine.

6. Bring the sauce to a boil, then reduce the heat to a simmer and continue cooking for 1 hour, stirring occasionally.

7. Stir in the water, basil, parsley, oregano, and sugar and cook for 15 more minutes. Taste the sauce and add salt and pepper as needed.

8. Remove the sauce from the heat and allow it to cool slightly before using it in the pasta. (Note: Sauce can be made up to 48 hours in advance. Cool completely, then cover and refrigerate until needed. Rewarm before using.)

9. In the meantime, bring a large pot of water to a rolling boil. Add a dash of salt, then add the pasta. Cook for 8 minutes, or until the pasta is al dente.

10. Drain the pasta well, then toss it into the Bolognese sauce. Serve warm, with the garlic bread, and sprinkled with oregano, Parmesan, and red pepper flakes.

continues on p. 89

GARLIC BREAD

5 heads garlic (pick the largest ones you can find)

¼ cup (50 ml) olive oil

¼ teaspoon salt

¼ teaspoon freshly ground black pepper

6 sprigs fresh thyme

1½ sticks (170 g) unsalted butter, room temperature

2 tablespoons (28 g) finely grated Parmesan cheese

2 tablespoons (20 g) finely chopped fresh parsley

1 teaspoon dried basil

¾ teaspoon onion powder

¼ teaspoon red pepper flakes

¼ teaspoon flaky sea salt

1 large loaf crusty bread, cut into 8 (1-inch) slices

Fresh oregano leaves, roughly chopped

Freshly grated Parmesan cheese

Red pepper flakes

FOR THE GARLIC BREAD

1. Preheat the oven to 400°F.
2. Cut the top from each head of garlic, making sure the top of each clove is exposed.
3. Place the heads of garlic on a large piece of heavy-duty aluminum foil, cut side up. Drizzle the oil over the garlic, then sprinkle with the salt, black pepper, and thyme.
4. Wrap the foil tightly around the garlic and place in a small baking dish.
5. Bake for 1 hour, turning the foil package upside down halfway through baking, or until garlic cloves are tender and easily pop out of their skin. Remove the foil package from the oven and set it aside until cool to the touch. Increase the oven temperature to 475°F.
6. Remove the garlic from the foil package and squeeze the lower part of the garlic heads to pop the cloves from their skins.
7. In the bowl of a stand mixer fitted with the paddle attachment, or in a large bowl using a handheld electric mixer, combine the roasted garlic, butter, Parmesan, parsley, basil, onion powder, pepper flakes, and sea salt. Beat on medium speed, scraping down the bowl as needed, until well combined.
8. Place the bread slices on a large baking sheet and toast for 3 minutes, flipping halfway through. Remove the bread from the oven and spread one side generously with the garlic butter.
9. Return the pan to the oven and bake for 5 minutes, or until golden brown. Serve warm.

Herb-Crusted Salmon with Mashed Potatoes | SERVES 6

When I worked at The Cheesecake Factory, my mom would often pop in and visit me for lunch. And she almost always ordered the same thing: herb-crusted salmon with mashed potatoes. On the rare occasion she didn't order it, she regretted it and was back a few days later to get her fix! So I decided to create a homemade version we could all enjoy any time the craving struck! Featuring thick salmon fillets covered in herbs and simply roasted, plus creamy homemade mashed potatoes, this recipe is what I like to think of as "lightened-up" comfort food.

HERB-CRUSTED SALMON

6 (6-ounce/170-g) fresh skin-on salmon fillets

2 tablespoons (28 ml) olive oil, divided

2 tablespoons (28 ml) country Dijon mustard

2 tablespoons (20 g) finely chopped fresh parsley

1 tablespoon (10 g) finely chopped fresh dill

1 tablespoon (10 g) finely chopped fresh tarragon leaves

1 tablespoon (10 g) finely chopped fresh chives

3 cloves garlic, minced

1 teaspoon salt

½ teaspoon freshly ground black pepper

2 lemons, quartered, seeds removed

Sprigs of fresh dill or parsley, for garnish (optional)

MASHED POTATOES

3 pounds (1.36 kg) russet potatoes, peeled and cut into quarters

½ cup (113 ml) whole milk

½ cup (113 ml) heavy cream

1 stick (113 g) unsalted butter

½ cup (113 g) sour cream

1 teaspoon salt, plus more to taste

½ teaspoon freshly ground black pepper, plus more to taste

1½ tablespoons (21 ml) olive oil

1 tablespoon (10 g) finely chopped fresh chives

1 tablespoon (10 g) finely chopped fresh parsley

FOR THE SALMON

1. Preheat the oven to 425°F. Line a large baking sheet with parchment paper.

2. Place the salmon fillets skin side down on the prepared baking sheet. Set the salmon aside.

3. In a small bowl, combine 1½ tablespoons (21 ml) of the oil with the mustard, herbs, garlic, salt, and pepper.

4. Divide the herb mixture evenly among the salmon fillets, spreading it evenly on top of each fillet. Scatter the lemons around the salmon fillets, and lightly drizzle with the remaining oil (7 ml).

5. Bake the salmon for 18 minutes, or until it is firm and flakes easily. (Note: This is a good time to get started on the mashed potatoes.)

6. Using a fish spatula, gently loosen the salmon fillets from their skin and arrange them on top of the mashed potatoes. Scatter the roasted lemons decoratively around the salmon and serve warm. Garnish with fresh dill and parsley, if desired.

FOR THE POTATOES

1. Place the potatoes in a large pot and cover with cold water 1 inch higher than the potatoes. Place the pot over high heat and bring to a rolling boil, then reduce the heat to medium-low and simmer for 15 minutes, or until the potatoes are very tender.

2. About 5 minutes before the potatoes are done cooking, combine the milk, cream, and butter in a small saucepan. Place over low heat and warm until the butter is completely melted. Keep over low heat until needed.

3. Drain the cooked potatoes, then return them to the pot. Pour the warm milk mixture over the potatoes, then add the sour cream, salt, and pepper. Mash until smooth, taking care not to over mash, which can make the potatoes gluey. Taste the potatoes and season with additional salt and pepper as needed.

4. Scrape the potatoes onto a large serving platter, drizzle with the oil, and sprinkle with the chives and parsley.

ASHLEY'S TIP

Good-quality salmon is key here! Fresh works best, and I recommend selecting pieces similar in shape and size so they cook evenly. If you don't have a specialty seafood shop, head to a grocery store seafood counter and ask them to help you select the best pieces.

4
CHAPTER

Sides

When it's time to gather around the holiday table and dig in, my first instinct is to head directly for the side dishes! This chapter focuses on crowd-pleasing soups and side dishes that are sure to enhance *any* holiday meal. But these recipes can also be made and enjoyed on their own or paired together to create mini meals! Pasta Fagioli and Parker House Rolls for dinner? Yes, please! Macaroni & Cheese and Caesar Salad for a quick weeknight meal? No complaints here! Mix and match these recipes to your heart's delight.

Rosemary & Garlic Roasted Potatoes | 94

Italian Wedding Soup | 97

Parker House Rolls | 98

Feel-Good Holiday Salad | 103

Pasta Fagioli | 104

Creamy White Cheddar Macaroni & Cheese | 107

Balsamic Roasted Brussels Sprouts with Pancetta & Pomegranate Seeds | 108

Crowd-Pleasing Caesar Salad with Garlic Bread Croutons | 111

Warm Bacon & Green Bean Salad | 115

Rosemary & Garlic Roasted Potatoes | SERVES 4 TO 6

Extra-crispy and covered in garlic and herbs: These potatoes are what dreams are made of! They will make your house smell incredible as they bake and can easily be paired with a variety of meals, from breakfast to dinner. I love serving them with quiche and a quick arugula salad for brunch, or alongside pancakes for breakfast for dinner.

¼ teaspoon baking soda

3 pounds (1.36 kg) red potatoes, diced into ¾-inch cubes

⅓ cup (67 ml) olive oil

2 tablespoons (20 g) fresh rosemary leaves, finely chopped

1¾ teaspoons garlic powder

1¼ teaspoons salt

½ teaspoon freshly ground black pepper

½ teaspoon granulated sugar

½ teaspoon onion powder

1. Preheat the oven to 425°F. Line a large baking sheet with parchment paper and set it aside. Line a large plate with several layers of paper towels and set it aside.

2. Bring a large pot of water to a boil. Add the baking soda—it will fizz up a good amount. Carefully add the potatoes and cook for 6 minutes, stirring occasionally.

3. Remove the pot from the heat and drain. Rinse the potatoes with cold water for 30 seconds. Then transfer the potatoes to the paper towel-lined plate and blot them dry using additional paper towels.

4. Transfer the potatoes to a large bowl and drizzle with the oil. Sprinkle on the rosemary, garlic powder, salt, pepper, sugar, and onion powder, and toss until the potatoes are evenly coated. Scatter the potatoes in a single layer on the prepared baking sheet.

5. Bake for 34 minutes, flipping them halfway through cooking. Then turn on the broiler and bake for 3 to 4 more minutes, or until they're well browned and crispy. Keep an eye on the potatoes, as it's easy to burn them when the broiler is on!

6. Cool for 5 minutes, then serve warm.

Italian Wedding Soup | SERVES 6 TO 8

One thing I've learned over the years is that you either know about Italian Wedding Soup—or you don't. There's no in between. Folks either grew up eating it and absolutely love it, or are utterly perplexed by the strange name and want to know "What makes it Italian?" and "Why is it called wedding soup?" To be honest, I don't have a solid answer to these questions. But the one thing I can tell you? This soup is soul-warming and absolutely delicious. Featuring mini meatballs, rich broth, tiny bits of pasta, and plenty of veggies, it's a guaranteed crowd-pleaser, and the funny name doubles as a great conversation starter!

MEATBALLS

8 ounces (227 g) ground sweet Italian sausage

8 ounces (227 g) ground beef

½ cup (25 g) panko breadcrumbs

1 large egg

1 teaspoon Italian seasoning

½ teaspoon garlic powder

½ teaspoon salt

½ teaspoon freshly ground black pepper

¼ cup (29 g) finely grated Parmesan cheese

3 tablespoons (42 ml) lukewarm water

SOUP

3 tablespoons (42 ml) olive oil

¼ teaspoon red pepper flakes

4 large carrots, peeled and chopped

3 stalks celery, finely chopped

1 large yellow onion, diced

8 cloves garlic, minced

8 cups (1.89 L) chicken broth

4 cups (907 ml) beef broth

1 cup (227 g) acini di pepe pasta

4 cups (about 141 g) lightly packed fresh spinach, roughly chopped

¾ teaspoon salt, plus more to taste

½ teaspoon freshly ground black pepper, plus more to taste

⅔ cup (66 g) finely grated Parmesan cheese, plus more for serving

3 tablespoons (42 ml) fresh lemon juice

Crusty bread, for serving

FOR THE MEATBALLS

1. Preheat the oven to 400°F. Line a large baking sheet with parchment paper and set it aside.

2. In a large bowl, combine the sausage, beef, breadcrumbs, egg, Italian seasoning, garlic powder, salt, pepper, and Parmesan. Add the water, mixing with your hands until just combined. (Don't overmix or the meatballs will be tough.) The mixture should be moist but still hold its shape when rolled into balls.

3. Using a small spoon, scoop out about 1½ teaspoons of the meat mixture and roll it into a ball. Place the ball on the prepared baking sheet. Repeat with the remaining meat mixture. You should have about 35 mini meatballs.

4. Bake the meatballs for 10 minutes. Remove the meatballs from the oven and set the pan aside. (Note: Meatballs can be made up to 48 hours in advance. Cool completely and store in an airtight container, in the refrigerator, until needed.)

FOR THE SOUP

1. In a large soup pot over medium heat, combine the oil, pepper flakes, carrots, celery, and onion. Cook for 5 to 6 minutes, stirring occasionally, or until tender.

2. Add the garlic and cook for 1 more minute, stirring frequently, or until fragrant. Don't let the garlic brown.

3. Add both broths. Increase the heat to medium-high and bring to a boil. Then reduce the heat to a simmer and cook for 30 minutes, stirring occasionally. Add the pasta and cook for 10 minutes, or until tender.

4. Stir in the baked meatballs, spinach, salt, and pepper. Cook until the spinach has wilted slightly, about 2 minutes. Stir in the Parmesan and lemon juice. Taste and season with additional salt and pepper as needed.

5. Serve warm, with crusty bread and extra Parmesan on the side. (Note: This soup will keep, stored in an airtight container in the refrigerator, for up to 48 hours. Reheat before serving.)

Parker House Rolls | YIELDS 24 ROLLS

I've eaten a lot of rolls in my life. And I must confess, most of them were a letdown. So, when I started working on this recipe, I was determined to make them extra special and "totally worth it." These golden-brown beauties are just that. They bake up light and fluffy, with a deeply colored lid that's just begging to be slathered in salted honey butter. (Oh yeah, I included a recipe for that, too!)

DOUGH

Nonstick cooking spray

1¼ cups (285 ml) warm whole milk (between 115° and 120° F)

1 stick (113 g) unsalted butter, melted

2 large eggs, room temperature

⅓ cup (67 g) granulated sugar

1 tablespoon (14 g) packed light brown sugar

1¾ teaspoons salt

1 (0.25-ounce/7 g) packet active dry yeast

4½ cups (540 g) bread flour, divided

TO ASSEMBLE

4 tablespoons (57 g) unsalted butter, melted, divided

1 large egg, room temperature

1 teaspoon whole milk

1 teaspoon flaky sea salt

FOR THE DOUGH

1. Lightly grease a large bowl with nonstick cooking spray and set it aside.

2. In the bowl of an electric stand mixer, whisk together the milk, butter, eggs, both sugars, salt, and yeast.

3. Add 2½ cups (300 g) of the flour and stir with a rubber spatula to form a shaggy dough. Place the bowl on the stand mixer and attach the dough hook.

4. With the mixer on medium-low speed, gradually add the remaining 2 cups (240 g) of flour, ¼ cup (30 g) at a time, until all the flour has been incorporated, and the dough is a uniform mass with no dry flour pockets. If any of the flour is sticking to the sides, stop the mixer and use a rubber spatula to mix it in, then continue kneading on medium-low speed.

5. Once all the flour has been added, increase the mixer speed to medium-high and continue kneading for 5 minutes, or until the dough is pulling away from the edges of the bowl and looks soft and smooth. The dough should feel elastic and slightly sticky to the touch.

6. Scrape the dough into the prepared bowl, cover with plastic wrap, and set aside for 90 minutes, or until the dough has puffed up and doubled in size.

TO ASSEMBLE

1. Grease a 9 x 13-inch ceramic or glass baking dish with 1 tablespoon (14 g) of the melted butter and set it aside.

2. Transfer the dough to a clean work surface and firmly press to release the air and deflate the dough. Using a sharp knife, divide the dough evenly in half (about 550 g per piece).

3. Roll one half of the dough out into a 24-inch rope. Press the rope flat to be 5 inches wide. Brush the surface lightly with 1 tablespoon (14 g) of melted butter.

4. Starting at the top long edge, fold one side of the dough in toward you, then fold the other side in to overlap it. Press at the seam and roll the dough over so it is seam side down. Carefully reshape as needed so that you have an even 24-inch rope of dough about 2 inches in width.

continues on p. 101

SALTED HONEY BUTTER

2 sticks (227 g) unsalted butter, room temperature

½ cup (170 ml) honey

1 teaspoon flaky sea salt

> **ASHLEY'S TIP**
>
> *This recipe requires patience and attention to detail. So read the recipe twice, make sure you have enough time for all the steps (including the inactive time), and double-check you have all ingredients called for. You've got this!*

5. Using a sharp knife, cut the dough into 12 (2-inch) pieces. Arrange the rolls, seam side down, in the prepared dish, making three rows of four rolls. Repeat with the remaining dough. *You will have 6 rows of 4 rolls, yielding 24 rolls in total.*

6. Cover the baking dish with plastic wrap and set aside for 60 to 75 minutes, or until the rolls have puffed up and almost doubled in size.

7. 30 minutes prior to baking, preheat the oven to 375°F.

8. In a small bowl, whisk together the egg and milk, beating until well combined. Brush the top of the rolls with the egg wash.

9. Bake for 25 minutes, rotating the pan at the halfway point, or until golden brown and the internal temperature reaches 200°F.

10. Brush the rolls with the remaining tablespoon (14 g) of melted butter and sprinkle with the sea salt.

11. Place the pan on a wire rack to cool for 20 minutes. Serve warm, with salted honey butter.

FOR THE HONEY BUTTER

1. In the bowl of a stand mixer fitted with the paddle attachment, or in a large bowl using a handheld electric mixer, beat the butter until smooth.

2. Add the honey and salt and beat on medium speed 3 to 4 minutes, or until completely smooth, scraping down the mixer and bowl with a spatula as needed.

3. Scrape into a small bowl and refrigerate for at least 30 minutes before serving. (Note: Salted Honey Butter will keep, covered and stored in the refrigerator, for up to 48 hours. If making ahead of time, allow the butter to soften at room temperature before serving.)

ASHLEY'S TIP

Unlike most recipes, salad is a place you can play around a bit. Feel free to get creative here and follow your instincts. Really love avocado? Double the amount! Hate blue cheese? Use feta, goat cheese, or Gorgonzola! Can't have nuts? Skip them!

Feel-Good Holiday Salad | SERVES 4 TO 6

I love indulging in life . . . especially during the holidays! I don't do diets, and I don't obsess over calories, carbs, or cardio. But like most people, I also like feeling good in my body. And that's where this vibrant holiday salad comes in. Loaded with nutrient-rich ingredients like avocado, spinach, arugula, and pomegranate seeds, it's a refreshing break from the typical ultra-rich holiday recipes. But rest assured, this salad is still crazy delicious! Bacon, blue cheese, and homemade balsamic dressing basically guarantee it! And the crunchy candied pecans make eating this salad feel like a total treat.

CANDIED PECANS

4 tablespoons (57 g) unsalted butter
¾ cup (149 g) granulated sugar
¼ cup (53 g) packed light brown sugar
¼ teaspoon salt
⅛ teaspoon cinnamon
1 large egg white
1 tablespoon (14 ml) water
2 teaspoons pure vanilla extract
16 ounces (454 g) pecan halves

DRESSING

½ cup (100 ml) olive oil
⅓ cup (76 ml) balsamic vinegar
2½ teaspoons pure maple syrup
1 teaspoon Dijon mustard
½ teaspoon salt, plus more to taste
¼ teaspoon freshly ground black pepper, plus more to taste

SALAD

8 ounces (227 g) sliced bacon
6 cups (about 275 g) lightly packed baby spinach
2 cups (about 75 g) lightly packed arugula
1 cup (140 g) fresh pomegranate arils
1 cup (127 g) crumbled blue cheese
¾ cup (106 g) dried cranberries
2 ripe avocados, diced

FOR THE PECANS

1. Preheat the oven to 300°F. In a small saucepan over medium heat, melt the butter. Pour the melted butter onto a large baking sheet and, using a pastry brush, spread it into an even layer. Set the baking sheet aside.

2. In a small bowl, combine both sugars, salt, and cinnamon. Set the bowl aside.

3. In a large bowl, whisk the egg white with the water and vanilla until the mixture is very frothy. Add the pecans to the egg white mixture and toss well to coat. Then add the sugar mixture and stir again, mixing until the pecans are evenly coated.

4. Spread the coated pecans onto the buttered baking sheet and bake, stirring every 15 minutes, for 1 hour. Cool pecans on the baking sheet for at least 30 minutes before serving. (Note: You will have more pecans than you'll need. Store leftovers in an airtight container, at room temperature, for up to 2 weeks.)

FOR THE DRESSING

1. Combine all the ingredients in a small jar. Secure the lid and shake vigorously, until the dressing is well combined. Taste and adjust seasoning as needed. Set the dressing aside.

FOR THE SALAD

1. Warm a large cast-iron skillet over medium heat. Add the bacon and cook 6 to 7 minutes, turning occasionally, until crisp and fully cooked. Transfer the bacon to a paper towel-lined plate. When cool enough to handle, roughly chop the cooked bacon and set it aside.

2. In a large salad bowl, toss together the spinach and arugula. Add 1 cup of the candied pecans and half of the pomegranate arils, blue cheese, cranberries, and bacon. Drizzle on one-third of the dressing and toss well to combine.

3. Top with the remaining pomegranate arils, blue cheese, cranberries, and bacon. Finally, add the avocado and a few more candied pecans on top. Serve at once, with the remaining dressing on the side.

Pasta Fagioli | SERVES 4 TO 6

As a die-hard pasta lover, this soup is my solution for nights when I can't decide if I should cook pasta or soup! Traditionally a hearty tomato-based soup loaded with pasta and beans, my version also includes sausage and plenty of veggies because . . . yum! I love serving this with extra Parmesan cheese, crusty bread, and a bold red wine. So cozy!

3 tablespoons (42 ml) olive oil

¼ teaspoon red pepper flakes

1 large yellow onion, chopped

1 pound (454 g) Italian sausage, casings removed (mild, sweet, or spicy)

4 large carrots, diced

6 cloves garlic, minced

½ teaspoon fresh thyme leaves, finely chopped

1 teaspoon Italian seasoning

4 cups (907 ml) chicken broth

2 (28-ounce/794-g) cans crushed tomatoes with basil

2 (15-ounce/439-g) cans white beans, drained and rinsed

¾ teaspoon salt, more to taste

½ teaspoon freshly ground black pepper, more to taste

1 cup (227 g) ditalini pasta

2½ cups (150 g) packed baby spinach, roughly chopped

Grated Parmesan cheese, for serving

1. In a large soup pot over medium heat warm the oil until shimmering. Add the pepper flakes and onion and cook for 6 minutes, stirring frequently, until soft and translucent.

2. Add the sausage and, using a wooden spoon, break it into small pieces. Cook until the sausage is brown and no pink remains.

3. Add the carrots and cook 5 to 6 minutes, or until slightly softened. Add the garlic, thyme, and Italian seasoning and cook for 1 to 2 minutes, stirring almost constantly, or until fragrant.

4. Pour in the broth and tomatoes and stir to combine. Increase the heat to medium-high and bring the soup to a boil. Then reduce to a simmer and cook for 40 minutes, stirring occasionally.

5. Stir in the beans, salt, and pepper and continue cooking for 10 more minutes.

6. In the meantime, bring a small pot of water to a rolling boil. Add a dash of salt, then add the pasta and cook for 7 to 8 minutes, or until al dente.

7. Drain the pasta well. Then toss the pasta into the soup. Stir in the spinach and cook for 2 minutes, or until the spinach has wilted slightly. Taste and season with additional salt and black pepper as needed.

8. Remove the soup from the heat and divide among serving bowls. Top with Parmesan and serve at once! (Note: This soup will keep, stored in an airtight container in the refrigerator, for up to 48 hours. Reheat before serving, and loosen the broth up with a little water or chicken broth, as needed.)

Creamy White Cheddar Macaroni & Cheese | SERVES 6 TO 8

Macaroni and cheese is the epitome of cozy winter comfort food. This homemade version, made with sharp cheddar, nutty Gruyère, and a lively variety of fresh herbs and spices is our family favorite! Panko breadcrumbs on top add just the right amount of crunch.

Nonstick cooking spray

½ teaspoon salt

1 pound (454 g) macaroni pasta

5 tablespoons (70 g) unsalted butter

4 shallots, diced

2 small cloves garlic, minced

1½ tablespoons (15 g) finely chopped fresh thyme leaves

¼ cup (30 g) all-purpose flour

3¾ cups (851 ml) whole milk

1 teaspoon fine sea salt, plus more to taste

½ teaspoon freshly ground black pepper, plus more to taste

½ teaspoon packed light brown sugar

¼ teaspoon cayenne pepper

¼ teaspoon ground nutmeg

⅓ cup (76 ml) heavy cream

16 ounces (454 g) sharp cheddar cheese, coarsely grated

6 ounces (170 g) Gruyère cheese, coarsely grated

¾ cup (38 g) panko breadcrumbs

1 tablespoon (14 ml) olive oil

1. Preheat the oven to 375°F. Lightly grease a 3-quart baking dish or cast-iron skillet with nonstick cooking spray and set it aside.

2. Bring a large pot of water to a boil over high heat. Add the salt and pasta and cook for 6 minutes. (The pasta will be very al dente.) Drain well, then pour the pasta into the prepared baking dish and set it aside.

3. In a large saucepan over medium heat, melt the butter. Add the shallots, garlic, and thyme and cook for 4 to 5 minutes, stirring frequently, until the shallots are softened and nearly translucent.

4. Slowly sprinkle in the flour, stirring constantly, and cook for 1 minute. Slowly pour in the milk, whisking constantly. Continue to cook, whisking almost constantly, until the mixture begins to thicken, about 6 minutes.

5. Whisk in the sea salt, black pepper, brown sugar, cayenne pepper, and nutmeg. Then remove the pan from the heat and immediately whisk in the cream.

6. Fold in the cheeses, mixing until evenly combined. Then pour the sauce over cooked pasta and stir gently to combine. Set it aside.

7. In a small bowl, combine the breadcrumbs and olive oil, mixing well with your hands, until the breadcrumbs are evenly coated. Sprinkle the breadcrumb mixture on top of the macaroni and cheese.

8. Bake for 22 to 24 minutes, or until the breadcrumbs are golden brown and the cheese is bubbling. Serve at once.

Balsamic Roasted Brussels Sprouts with Pancetta & Pomegranate Seeds | SERVES 4 TO 6

Think Brussels sprouts are boring? Or even worse... gross? I beg you to think again and give this ultra-flavorful recipe a chance to change your mind. Baked until golden brown, dressed in a balsamic-maple sauce, and topped with crunchy pomegranate seeds and pancetta, this pretty dish packs a punch!

DRESSING

8 ounces (227 g) pancetta, diced
3 tablespoons (42 ml) olive oil
3 tablespoons (42 ml) balsamic vinegar
1½ tablespoons (29 ml) pure maple syrup
1½ teaspoons Dijon mustard
3 cloves garlic, minced
¼ teaspoon salt, plus more to taste
¼ teaspoon freshly ground black pepper, plus more to taste

ROASTED BRUSSELS SPROUTS

3½ pounds fresh Brussels sprouts, trimmed and cut in half
¼ cup (50 ml) olive oil
1½ teaspoons balsamic vinegar
¾ teaspoon salt
½ teaspoon freshly ground black pepper
¼ teaspoon red pepper flakes
¼ teaspoon garlic powder
1 cup (142 g) pomegranate arils

FOR THE DRESSING

1. Line a large plate with two layers of paper towels. Set it aside.

2. In a medium skillet over medium heat cook the pancetta, stirring occasionally, until the fat renders and the pancetta is golden brown and crispy. Transfer the cooked pancetta to the prepared plate and set it aside.

3. In a large bowl, whisk together the oil, vinegar, maple syrup, mustard, garlic, salt, and pepper. Whisk well, until the mixture is evenly combined. Taste and adjust salt and pepper as needed. Set the dressing aside.

FOR THE BRUSSELS SPROUTS

1. Preheat the oven to 425°F. Line a large baking sheet with parchment paper and set it aside.

2. In a large bowl, combine the Brussels sprouts, olive oil, vinegar, salt, black pepper, pepper flakes, and garlic powder. Toss well to coat.

3. Scatter the Brussels sprouts in a single layer on the prepared baking sheet.

4. Bake for 15 minutes. Then flip the brussels sprouts and increase the oven temperature to 475°F. Continue baking for 10 to 12 minutes, or until the Brussels sprouts are golden brown with slightly darker brown spots.

5. Carefully remove the pan from the oven. Add the Brussels sprouts to the dressing bowl and toss well to combine.

6. Place on a serving platter and sprinkle with the cooked pancetta and pomegranate arils. Serve at once.

Crowd-Pleasing Caesar Salad with Garlic Bread Croutons | SERVES 4 TO 6

This classic crowd-pleasing salad will always have a place on my table. Like most Caesar salads, it's loaded with a creamy dressing and topped with Parmesan cheese and croutons. So, what makes this one so special? Homemade dressing and garlic bread croutons! These two little twists take this salad from good to great.

GARLIC BREAD CROUTONS

5 tablespoons (70 g) unsalted butter, melted

2 small cloves garlic, minced

1 French-style baguette, ends trimmed and discarded, cut into ½-inch cubes

2½ tablespoons (35 ml) olive oil

½ tablespoon (5 g) finely chopped fresh rosemary leaves

¾ teaspoon garlic powder

¼ teaspoon salt

¼ teaspoon freshly ground black pepper

¼ teaspoon onion powder

¼ teaspoon Italian seasoning

¼ cup (28 g) finely grated Parmesan cheese

CAESAR DRESSING

2 tablespoons (28 ml) olive oil

1½ tablespoons (21 ml) lemon juice

1½ tablespoons (21 ml) red wine vinegar

1½ tablespoons (21 ml) Worcestershire sauce

1 tablespoon (14 g) capers, drained

1 tablespoon (10 g) roughly chopped fresh parsley

1 tablespoon (14 g) Dijon mustard

1 teaspoon garlic powder

½ teaspoon finely grated lemon zest

½ teaspoon anchovy paste, more to taste

¼ teaspoon granulated sugar

¼ teaspoon freshly ground black pepper

FOR THE CROUTONS

1. Preheat the oven to 350°F. In a small saucepan over medium-low heat melt the butter. Add the garlic and cook for 1 minute, stirring frequently. Do not let it brown. Remove the pan from the heat and set it aside.

2. In a large bowl, add the bread cubes and drizzle with the butter mixture. Add the oil, rosemary, garlic powder, salt, pepper, onion powder, Italian seasoning, and Parmesan. Toss well to ensure the bread cubes are evenly coated.

3. Spread the bread cubes out in an even layer on a large baking sheet. If you can't fit them in one layer, use two baking sheets—don't crowd them.

4. Bake the bread cubes for 14 minutes, flipping halfway through, or until golden brown and crispy. Place the baking sheet on a wire rack and cool completely, about 1 hour. You will have more croutons than you'll need. Store leftovers in an airtight container, at room temperature, for up to 1 week.

FOR THE DRESSING

1. In the bowl of a small food processor or blender, combine the oil, lemon juice, vinegar, Worcestershire, capers, parsley, mustard, garlic powder, lemon zest, anchovy paste, sugar, black pepper, and garlic cloves and pulse until smooth. Set the mixture aside.

2. In a medium bowl, whisk together the mayonnaise and Parmesan, mixing until smooth. Slowly pour in the garlic vinaigrette, whisking constantly, until completely combined. Taste and adjust seasoning as needed.

3. Use at once or cover and store in the refrigerator for up to 24 hours Mix well before serving.

continues on p. 112

2 to 3 small cloves garlic, minced, to taste

1 cup (227 g) good-quality mayonnaise

⅓ cup (50 g) finely grated Parmesan cheese

SALAD

4 heads (16 ounces/454 g) romaine hearts, roughly chopped

2 cups (142 g) croutons, plus more to taste

½ cup (50 g) freshly shaved Parmesan cheese, plus more to taste

6 anchovy fillets, plus more to taste (optional)

Freshly ground black pepper (optional)

FOR THE SALAD

1. Place the romaine in a large bowl. Add the salad dressing, 1 cup (71 g) of the croutons, and half of the Parmesan (25 g) and toss well to combine.
2. Top with the remaining cheese, anchovies (if using), the remaining 1 cup (71 g) of croutons, and freshly ground black pepper (if using). Serve at once.

Warm Bacon & Green Bean Salad | SERVES 4 TO 6

Say hello to my favorite way to eat green beans! This warm salad features perfectly cooked green beans tossed in a flavor-packed vinaigrette and topped with crunchy walnuts and crispy bits of bacon.

1 pound (454 g) French green beans, trimmed

½ cup (57 g) walnuts, toasted

8 ounces (227 g) sliced bacon

1 medium yellow onion, finely chopped

⅓ cup (76 ml) apple cider vinegar

2 tablespoons (28 g) Dijon mustard

2 tablespoons (28 g) packed brown sugar

1 tablespoon (14 g) granulated sugar

¾ teaspoon salt

½ teaspoon freshly ground black pepper

1. Make an ice bath by filling a large bowl halfway with ice, then add very cold water until the bowl is three-quarters full. Set the bowl aside until needed.

2. Bring a large pot of water to a rolling boil. Add the green beans and cook for 4 minutes. Using a slotted spoon, remove them from the boiling water and immediately plunge them into the ice bath. Drain the green beans once they are cool, then pat them dry. Set them aside.

3. In a large skillet over medium heat toast the walnuts for 3 to 4 minutes, stirring frequently, until fragrant and one shade darker in color. Take care not to burn them. Remove the walnuts from the skillet and cool. Roughly chop the toasted nuts and set them aside.

4. Carefully wipe the skillet clean, then place it back over medium heat. Add the bacon and cook 6 to 7 minutes, turning occasionally, until crisp and fully cooked. Transfer the bacon to a paper towel-lined plate. When cool enough to handle, roughly chop the cooked bacon and set it aside.

5. Carefully remove about 1 tablespoon (14 ml) of the bacon grease from the skillet, then place it back over medium heat. Add the onion to the skillet and cook 5 to 6 minutes, stirring occasionally, until soft and translucent.

6. In the meantime, in a large glass measuring cup, combine the vinegar, mustard, both sugars, salt, and pepper and whisk until well combined. Pour the dressing into the skillet and cook for 3 minutes, stirring occasionally, or until bubbling and slightly thickened.

7. Add ¼ cup of the chopped bacon and the green beans and toss to coat. Cook for 4 minutes, then transfer to a serving dish. Top with the remaining bacon and walnuts. Lightly toss, if desired, and serve at once.

5
CHAPTER

Desserts

"A party without a cake is just a meeting." —Julia Child

Well said, Julia! Well said. And I truly believe the same sentiment can be applied to any holiday event without dessert. So in this chapter you'll find showstopping layer cakes, cheesecakes, cupcakes, and more. These sweet endings are perfect for celebrations big and small!

Eggnog Tiramisu | 118

New York–Style Cheesecake with Grand Marnier® Cranberry Sauce | 121

Extra-Creamy Cannoli | 125

Chocolate Peppermint Cake | 126

Pumpkin Cheesecake with Pecan Praline Sauce | 129

Christmas Funfetti Sheet Cake | 133

Black Forest Cheesecake | 137

Sparkling Champagne Cupcakes | 141

Cranberry Cherry Pie | 145

Gingerbread Celebration Cake | 149

Eggnog Tiramisu | YIELDS ONE 9 X 13-INCH TIRAMISU (ABOUT 12 SLICES)

Here we combine two of my all-time favorite holiday treats: eggnog and tiramisu! The base of tiramisu uses a ton of egg yolks, so it was easy to transform the flavor with a dash of nutmeg and a little dark brandy. But if you prefer bourbon or cognac, go ahead and use it! The flavors and textures in this recipe improve with time, so it's a great dessert to make the day before you plan to serve it.

9 large egg yolks, room temperature

½ cup (99 g) granulated sugar

¼ cup (57 ml) dark rum

¼ teaspoon salt

16 ounces (454 g) mascarpone cheese, room temperature

¼ teaspoon ground nutmeg

1½ cups (340 ml) heavy cream, cold

2 tablespoons (14 g) confectioners' sugar

2 cups (454 ml) freshly brewed strong coffee, hot

1½ ounces (42 g) 70% dark chocolate, finely chopped

¼ cup (57 ml) Kahlúa liqueur

2 teaspoons pure vanilla extract

48 hard ladyfingers

Unsweetened cocoa powder, for dusting

1. Fill a medium saucepan one-third full with water and bring it to a low simmer over moderate heat. Reduce the heat to low.

2. In a large glass heatproof bowl that fits snugly on top of the saucepan, add the egg yolks and granulated sugar. Using a handheld electric mixer, beat on high speed until the mixture is thick and pale yellow, 3 to 4 minutes. Decrease the mixer speed to low and add the rum and salt, beating until combined.

3. Place the bowl on top of the saucepan, ensuring the bottom of the bowl does not touch the water. Then, using the electric mixer, beat the mixture until very thick, and its temperature registers 145°F on an instant-read thermometer. This can take about 10 minutes, so be patient and don't stop mixing (or the mixture may curdle).

4. Carefully remove the bowl from the heat and add the mascarpone, a little bit at a time, beating on low speed until the mixture is smooth, and the cheese is completely incorporated. Whisk in the nutmeg. Set the bowl aside for 15 minutes, or until the mixture has cooled.

5. In the meantime, in a large chilled bowl, combine the cream and confectioners' sugar and, using a handheld electric mixer, beat on medium speed until soft peaks form. Using a rubber spatula, gradually fold the whipped cream into the cooled mascarpone mixture, stirring well to combine. Set it aside.

6. In a large bowl, combine the hot coffee and chocolate and whisk until the chocolate is completely melted. Then whisk in the Kahlúa and vanilla.

7. Quickly dip half of the ladyfingers, one at a time, into the coffee mixture, and arrange them in a single layer on the bottom of a 9 x 13-inch baking dish. (Take care not to soak the ladyfingers too long, or the tiramisu will be soggy.) Spread half of the mascarpone cream mixture (about 520 g) on top of the ladyfingers and smooth the top with a spatula.

8. Repeat with a second layer of coffee-dipped ladyfingers, then top with the remaining mascarpone cream. Dust lightly with cocoa powder, then wrap the pan tightly with plastic wrap, making sure to keep it from touching the surface of the tiramisu.

9. Refrigerate the tiramisu for at least 8 hours (or up to 24 hours) before serving. Dust with more cocoa powder, if desired, right before serving.

New York-Style Cheesecake with Grand Marnier® Cranberry Sauce | YIELDS ONE 9-INCH CHEESECAKE

If you're a cheesecake purist, you're going to love this recipe! Featuring a crunchy graham cracker crust and dense but creamy cheesecake filling, it's a timeless classic! I could have stopped there . . . but instead, I made an eye-catching cranberry sauce, spiked it with Grand Marnier®, and spooned it all over the cheesecake. Can you tell I'm a more is more kind of gal?

CRUST

Nonstick baking spray

2 cups (210 g) graham cracker crumbs

⅓ cup (67 g) granulated sugar

7 tablespoons (99 g) unsalted butter, melted

CHEESECAKE FILLING

40 ounces (1.13 kg) full-fat cream cheese, room temperature

1 cup (227 g) full-fat sour cream, room temperature

1½ cups (298 g) granulated sugar

2 teaspoons pure vanilla extract

5 large eggs plus 3 egg yolks, room temperature

¼ cup (57 ml) heavy cream, room temperature

1 tablespoon (7 g) all-purpose flour

FOR THE CRUST

1. Preheat the oven to 350°F. Lightly grease a 9-inch springform pan with nonstick baking spray. Wrap the bottom and sides of the pan with extra-wide heavy duty aluminum foil. (I recommend using several layers to ensure no water seeps in when the pan is in the water bath.)

2. In a large bowl, mix the graham cracker crumbs, sugar, and butter together until well combined. Press the graham cracker mixture into the prepared pan, pressing down firmly across the bottom and about ½ inch up the sides.

3. Bake the crust for 10 minutes. Place the partially baked crust on a wire rack and set it aside while you prepare the filling.

FOR THE FILLING

1. In the bowl of a food processor or in a very large bowl using a handheld electric mixer, beat the cream cheese and sour cream until completely smooth, scraping down the bowl as needed. Add the sugar and vanilla and beat until smooth.

2. On low speed, add the eggs and egg yolks, one at a time, beating just until combined. (Do not overmix; if too much air is incorporated into the batter, it will rise in the oven, and then fall as it cools.)

3. Add the heavy cream and beat on low speed until completely incorporated into the batter. Fold in the flour, mixing just until combined.

4. Pour the filling on top of the partially baked crust and, using a rubber spatula, smooth the top. Place the cheesecake into a large, deep pan. Then fill the pan with 3 inches of hot water to create a water bath. (This helps ensure the cheesecake comes out crack-free.)

5. Carefully place the pan in the oven and bake for 30 minutes. Then reduce the temperature to 300°F and continue baking for 40 minutes.

6. Turn the oven off and let the cheesecake sit, undisturbed, for 40 minutes, inside the oven with the door shut. The cheesecake should still be slightly wiggly.

continues on p. 122

GRAND MARNIER® CRANBERRY SAUCE

½ cup (113 ml) fresh orange juice

¼ cup (57 ml) water

½ cup (106 g) packed dark brown sugar

⅓ cup (67 g) granulated sugar

12 ounces (347 g) cranberries, fresh or frozen (if frozen, do not thaw)

1 teaspoon finely grated orange zest

2 tablespoons (28 g) Grand Marnier®

2 teaspoons pure vanilla extract

7. Remove the cheesecake from the oven and gently run a knife around the edge of the cake. Place the cheesecake pan on a wire rack and cool completely. Then loosely cover the pan with plastic wrap and chill in the refrigerator for at least 8 hours. (Note: The cheesecake should be fully chilled before removing the springform pan.)

8. The cheesecake will keep, covered in the refrigerator, for 5 days, or wrapped tightly and frozen, for 2 months. If freezing, thaw overnight in the refrigerator before slicing.

FOR THE SAUCE

1. In a medium saucepan over medium-high heat, whisk together the orange juice, water, and both sugars. Bring to a boil and cook for 5 minutes, stirring occasionally. Add the cranberries and orange zest and stir well to combine.

2. Reduce the heat to a simmer and continue cooking, stirring occasionally and lightly smashing some of the cranberries, for 10 minutes.

3. Remove the pan from the heat. Stir in the Grand Marnier® and vanilla until well combined. (Note: Grand Marnier® may be substituted with another orange liqueur or omitted completely.)

4. Pour the sauce into a bowl and cool to room temperature. Then chill the sauce in the refrigerator until cold, about 2 hours. (Note: Sauce can be made up to 24 hours in advance. Cool completely and store in an airtight container, in the refrigerator, until needed. Stir well before using.)

5. Spoon the sauce over the cheesecake right before serving.

Extra-Creamy Cannoli | YIELDS 12 CANNOLI

My secret to extra-creamy cannoli? Blend the filling in a food processor. This little trick eliminates any grittiness and creates a silky-smooth filling that's truly divine! I have to warn you, these fly off dessert platters, so if you're serving a crowd, you might want to double the batch. I've seen guests go back for seconds and even thirds!

- 16 ounces (454 g) whole-milk ricotta cheese
- 8 ounces (227 g) full-fat cream cheese, room temperature
- 8 ounces (227 g) mascarpone cheese, room temperature
- 1½ cups (170 g) confectioners' sugar, sifted, divided
- 1 teaspoon pure vanilla extract
- ½ teaspoon orange blossom water (optional)
- 12 large cannoli shells
- 1 cup (173 g) mini chocolate chips
- 1 cup (150 g) roughly chopped unsalted pistachios (pick out any brown or dull green nuts and only use the vibrant green nuts)

1. Place a fine-mesh strainer over a large bowl, with at least 2 inches of space between the bottom of the strainer and the bottom of the bowl.
2. Line the strainer with three long layers of cheesecloth. Scrape the ricotta into the cheesecloth and fold the cheesecloth around the ricotta. Twist the top of the cheesecloth into makeshift handles and gently nestle them on top of the cheese ball. Place weights, such as a heavy can or a resealable bag full of pie weights or rice, on top of the ricotta and press down gently.
3. Refrigerate the cheese for at least 4 hours, or overnight if time permits. The longer you refrigerate, the more time your cheese will have to drain.
4. Remove the bowl from the refrigerator and remove the weights. Use the cheesecloth "handles" to lift the cheese out of the strainer. Then gently twist the cheesecloth and softly squeeze to press any remaining liquid from the cheese. Repeat as needed.
5. In the bowl of a food processor, combine the strained ricotta, cream cheese, mascarpone, and 1¼ cups (141 g) of the confectioners' sugar. Beat until smooth, stopping the processor and scraping the sides and bottom of the bowl a few times. Add the vanilla and orange blossom water (if using) and pulse for another minute, or until well combined.
6. Line a fine-mesh strainer with two layers of cheesecloth, then place the strainer snugly on top of a large bowl. Scrape the filling into the strainer and refrigerate for at least 2 hours, and up to 24 hours.
7. When ready to serve, scrape the filling into a large piping bag fitted with a large round open piping tip.
8. Pipe the filling into one end of a cannoli shell until it reaches the halfway point of the shell. Then fill the other end. Be sure to generously fill the shells so that the filling comes all the way to the end of each cannoli shell. Repeat with all shells.
9. Dip the ends of each cannolo in the chocolate chips or pistachios. I recommend doing half of each so your guests have variety. Lightly dust with the remaining ¼ cup (29 g) of confectioners' sugar and serve at once!

ASHLEY'S TIP

You can find cannoli shells at most major chain grocery stores. My favorite brand is Bellino. If you can't find them, try your local Italian market or bakery and ask if they'll sell you a box of shells. Most will! You can also order cannoli shells online from a variety of websites, including DeLallo.com, which offers them in full size and minis. In a pinch, you can serve this as a dip, with broken-up waffle cones or pizzelles.

Chocolate Peppermint Cake | YIELDS ONE 9-INCH LAYER CAKE

Peppermint mocha lattes are my favorite holiday coffee drink. And this cake is my love letter to that flavor combination. Featuring three layers of ultra-moist chocolate cake, white chocolate buttercream, and chocolate ganache, this dessert is a showstopper!

CHOCOLATE PEPPERMINT CAKE

Nonstick baking spray

1½ cups (298 g) granulated sugar

1½ cups (319 g) packed light brown sugar

2½ cups (300 g) all-purpose flour

1¾ cups (148 g) unsweetened cocoa powder, sifted

2 teaspoons baking soda

1 teaspoon baking powder

1 teaspoon salt

3 large eggs plus 2 egg yolks, room temperature

1½ cups (340 ml) whole milk, room temperature

¾ cup (150 ml) vegetable oil

⅓ cup (76 g) full-fat sour cream, room temperature

1¼ teaspoons peppermint extract

1 teaspoon pure vanilla extract

2 teaspoons espresso powder

1½ cups (340 ml) boiling water

WHITE CHOCOLATE PEPPERMINT FROSTING

4 sticks (454 g) unsalted butter, room temperature

4½ cups (513 g) confectioners' sugar, sifted

3½ tablespoons (49 ml) whole milk

1¼ teaspoons peppermint extract

½ teaspoon salt

8 ounces (227 g) white chocolate, melted and cooled for 10 minutes

FOR THE CAKE

1. Preheat the oven to 350°F. Line the bottoms of three 9-inch cake pans with parchment paper rounds, then grease the pans and paper with nonstick baking spray. Set the pans aside.

2. In a large bowl, whisk both sugars, flour, cocoa powder, baking soda, baking powder, and salt together until well combined, breaking up any chunks of brown sugar or cocoa powder.

3. In another large bowl, whisk the eggs and egg yolks, milk, oil, sour cream, peppermint extract, and vanilla together until well combined.

4. Pour the wet ingredients into the dry ingredients and using a rubber spatula, mix just until evenly combined. Avoid overmixing.

5. In a large glass measuring cup, combine the espresso powder and boiling water. Allow the mixture to sit for 30 seconds, then whisk until combined. Fold into the batter, mixing until evenly combined, about 30 seconds. The batter will be thin.

6. Divide the batter evenly among the prepared pans (about 720 g per pan).

7. Bake the cakes for 25 minutes, or until a toothpick or cake tester inserted in the center comes out clean or with a few moist crumbs attached.

8. Transfer the pans to wire racks and cool for 10 minutes. Then invert the cakes onto the racks and cool completely.

FOR THE FROSTING

1. In the bowl of a stand mixer fitted with the paddle attachment, or in a large bowl using a handheld electric mixer, beat the butter on medium speed until completely smooth. Reduce the speed to low, and gradually add the confectioners' sugar, beating until the sugar is completely incorporated.

2. Add the milk, peppermint extract, and salt and beat until smooth.

3. Add the white chocolate and beat until smooth, scraping down the bottom and sides of the bowl as needed. Increase the speed to medium-high and beat for 1 to 2 minutes, or until smooth and super fluffy.

continues on p. 128

CHOCOLATE GANACHE

8 ounces (227 g) 72% dark chocolate, finely chopped

1 cup (227 ml) heavy cream

1 teaspoon espresso powder

2 tablespoons (28 ml) Kahlúa liqueur

¼ teaspoon peppermint extract

1 cup (177 g) crushed candy canes

FOR THE GANACHE

1. Place the chocolate in a medium heatproof bowl.

2. In a small saucepan warm the cream over medium heat just until it begins to simmer and bubble, but does not come to a full boil, about 2 minutes. Whisk in the espresso powder.

3. Pour the cream mixture over the chocolate. Let the chocolate and cream stand untouched for 1 minute, then vigorously whisk together until the chocolate melts and a smooth ganache has formed, about 1 minute.

4. Whisk in the Kahlúa and peppermint extract. Allow the ganache to cool for about 10 minutes, or until it's cool but can still be easily drizzled from a spoon.

TO ASSEMBLE

1. Fit a large piping bag with an open star tip. Scrape about 1 cup (about 250 g) of the white chocolate peppermint frosting into the bag and set it aside.

2. Using a long-serrated knife, carefully trim the raised top of each cake, giving each one an even, level surface.

3. Transfer one cake layer to a large plate or cake stand. Spread a thick layer of frosting evenly on top, then top with another cake layer, and repeat, thickly spreading with frosting. Top with the final cake layer and use the remaining frosting to cover the top and sides of the cake.

4. Slowly and gradually, spoon some of the ganache around the top edges of the cake. Using a small spoon, gently push the ganache over the edge, allowing it to spill down the sides. Go slowly here and push only a small amount at a time to create delicate, pretty drips. Allow the ganache to fully set before topping with piped frosting and garnishes, about 20 minutes.

5. Pipe stars of the reserved frosting around the cake, however you would like.

6. Before serving, decorate with the crushed candy canes! Sprinkle them on top and press them on the sides of the cake, or as desired.

ASHLEY'S TIP

Bake and freeze the cake layers up to 2 months in advance. Bake cakes as directed and cool completely. Then wrap each cake layer in plastic wrap, then wrap in two layers of aluminum foil. Place the cakes in the freezer, somewhere they are safe and secure. When ready to use, allow the layers to thaw in the refrigerator for 12 to 24 hours. Remove the wrapping and assemble as directed.

Pumpkin Cheesecake with Pecan Praline Sauce | YIELDS ONE 9-INCH CHEESECAKE

Can't decide between pumpkin pie and pecan pie? I say skip both and make this crazy delicious hybrid cheesecake instead! The cheesecake filling is silky smooth and explodes with pumpkin pie flavor. And the pecan praline sauce adds just the right amount of crunch and tastes just like pecan pie filling. What's not to love?

GRAHAM CRACKER CRUST

Nonstick baking spray

2 cups (210 g) graham cracker crumbs

⅓ cup (67 g) granulated sugar

½ teaspoon pumpkin pie spice

¼ teaspoon salt

7 tablespoons (99 g) unsalted butter, melted

PUMPKIN CHEESECAKE FILLING

24 ounces (681 g) full-fat cream cheese, room temperature

½ cup (113 g) full-fat sour cream, room temperature

15 ounces (425 g) canned pumpkin puree

1 cup (213 g) packed dark brown sugar

½ cup (99 g) granulated sugar

3 large eggs plus 2 egg yolks, room temperature

2 tablespoons (15 g) all-purpose flour

2 teaspoons pure vanilla extract

2 teaspoons pumpkin pie spice

1 teaspoon ground cinnamon

½ teaspoon ground ginger

¼ teaspoon ground allspice

⅛ teaspoon ground cloves

⅛ teaspoon ground nutmeg

FOR THE CRUST

1. Preheat the oven to 350°F. Lightly grease a 9-inch springform pan with nonstick baking spray. Wrap the bottom and sides of the pan well with several layers of extra-wide heavy-duty aluminum foil. (This is to ensure no water seeps in when the pan is in the water bath.)

2. In a large bowl, mix the graham cracker crumbs, sugar, pumpkin pie spice, salt, and butter together until well combined.

3. Press the graham cracker mixture into the prepared pan, pressing down firmly across the bottom and about ½ inch up the sides.

4. Bake the crust for 10 minutes. Place the partially baked crust on a wire rack and set it aside while you prepare the filling. Reduce the oven to 325°F.

FOR THE FILLING

1. In the bowl of a food processor or in a large bowl using a handheld electric mixer, beat the cream cheese and sour cream until completely smooth, scraping down the bowl as needed. Add the pumpkin puree and both sugars and beat until smooth.

2. On low speed, add the eggs and egg yolks, one at a time, beating just until combined. (Don't overmix; if too much air is incorporated into the batter, it will rise in the oven and fall as it cools.)

3. Add the flour, vanilla, and all the spices and slowly pulse for another 20 seconds, or just until the flour has completely disappeared into the batter.

4. Pour the filling on top of the partially baked crust and, using a rubber spatula, smooth the top.

5. Place the cheesecake into a large deep pan. Then fill the pan with 3 inches of hot water to create a water bath. (This helps ensure the cheesecake comes out crack-free.)

6. Carefully place the pan in the oven and bake for 30 minutes, then reduce the temperature to 300°F and continue baking for another 55 minutes.

7. Turn the oven off and let the cheesecake sit, undisturbed, for 40 minutes, inside the oven with the door shut. The cheesecake should still be slightly wiggly.

continues on p. 130

PECAN PRALINE TOPPING

6 tablespoons (85 g) unsalted butter

¾ cup (159 g) packed dark brown sugar

⅓ cup (76 ml) heavy cream

½ teaspoon ground cinnamon

¼ teaspoon salt

2 cups (227 g) pecans, roughly chopped

1 tablespoon (14 ml) bourbon, optional

1 teaspoon pure vanilla extract

8. Remove cheesecake from the oven and gently run a knife around the edge of the cake. Place the cheesecake pan on a wire rack and cool completely. Then loosely cover the pan with plastic wrap and chill in the refrigerator for at least 8 hours, or up to 5 days. (Note: The cheesecake should be fully chilled before removing the springform pan.)

FOR THE TOPPING

1. In a large skillet over low heat, melt the butter. Add the brown sugar and cook, stirring with a whisk, until the sugar has melted and mixture is bubbling, about 2 minutes.

2. Add the cream, cinnamon, and salt and whisk to combine. Add the pecans and, using a rubber spatula, fold them into the liquid mixture until completely coated. Remove the pan from the heat and stir in the bourbon (if using) and vanilla.

3. Transfer to a large bowl and cool completely, at room temperature, about 30 minutes, stirring occasionally.

4. Spread the topping over the chilled cheesecake. Slice and serve.

ASHLEY'S TIP

The pecan praline topping is best served fresh but can be made up to 24 hours in advance. Store in a microwave safe container, in the refrigerator. Right before serving, microwave for 20 to 30 seconds, or just until it's gooey and pourable.

The cheesecake will keep, covered in the refrigerator, for 5 days, or wrapped tightly and frozen, for 2 months. If freezing, thaw overnight in the refrigerator before slicing.

Christmas Funfetti Sheet Cake | YIELDS ONE 9 X 13-INCH SHEET CAKE

I grew up on Funfetti cake, which is essentially just white cake with lots and lots of rainbow sprinkles baked inside! It's such a happy-looking dessert that I decided to make a Christmas version using red, green, and white sprinkles. If you don't celebrate Christmas, feel free to use any color of sprinkles that excites you! Just be sure to use sprinkles (also known as jimmies in some places) in the cake batter, and not nonpareils! Nonpareils will bleed into the batter. They can, however, be used on top of the frosting as additional decor.

SHEET CAKE

Nonstick baking spray

3 cups (360 g) cake flour

2½ teaspoons baking powder

½ teaspoon baking soda

½ teaspoon salt

2 sticks (227 g) unsalted butter, room temperature

1½ cups (298 g) granulated sugar

6 large egg whites, room temperature, beaten until frothy

¾ cup (170 ml) whole milk, room temperature

¾ cup (170 g) full-fat sour cream, room temperature

¼ cup (50 ml) vegetable oil

1 tablespoon (14 ml) pure vanilla extract

½ cup (85 g) red, green, and white sprinkles, plus more for decorating (do not use nonpareils!)

FOR THE CAKE

1. Preheat the oven to 350°F. Line a 9 x 13-inch baking pan with parchment paper. Grease the parchment paper, and any exposed pan, with nonstick baking spray. Set the pan aside.

2. In a large bowl, sift together the flour, baking powder, baking soda, and salt. Set the bowl aside.

3. In the bowl of a stand mixer fitted with the paddle attachment, or in a large bowl using a handheld electric mixer, beat the butter on medium speed for 1 minute, until smooth and creamy.

4. Gradually add the sugar, beating until smooth after each addition, and scraping down the bottom and sides of the bowl as needed. Once all the sugar has been added, increase speed to medium-high and beat about 2 minutes until light and fluffy. Turn the mixer off and scrape down the sides and bottom of the bowl, then beat on medium speed for another 10 seconds.

5. Reduce mixer speed to medium-low. Add the egg whites in three additions, beating well after each addition, and turning off the mixer and scraping down the sides and bottom of the bowl as needed.

6. In a large glass measuring cup with a spout, whisk together the milk, sour cream, oil, and vanilla.

7. With the mixer on the lowest speed, add the flour mixture in three additions, alternating with the sour cream mixture in two additions, beginning and ending with the flour mixture, and mixing until just combined.

8. Using a rubber spatula, gently fold in the sprinkles, mixing just until they're evenly distributed in the batter.

9. Pour the batter into the prepared baking pan and use a spatula to gently smooth the top. Bake for 32 to 35 minutes, or until the top is firm, golden brown, and a toothpick inserted in the middle of the cake comes out clean, or with a few moist crumbs attached.

10. Transfer the pan to a wire rack. Cool the cake in the pan completely before frosting.

continues on p. 134

CREAM CHEESE FROSTING

- 8 ounces (227 g) full-fat cream cheese, room temperature
- 6 tablespoons (85 g) unsalted butter, room temperature
- 3 cups (342 g) confectioners' sugar, sifted
- 1 tablespoon (14 ml) whole milk, plus more as needed
- ½ teaspoon pure vanilla extract
- ¼ teaspoon salt
- 2 tablespoons red, green, and white nonpareil sprinkles, for decorating (do not use these in the cake!)

FOR THE FROSTING

1. In the bowl of a stand mixer fitted with the paddle attachment, or in a large bowl using a handheld electric mixer, beat the cream cheese and butter on medium speed until smooth and creamy.
2. Reduce the speed to low and gradually add the confectioners' sugar, beating well after each addition. Add the milk, vanilla, and salt and beat until smooth.
3. Increase the speed to medium-high and beat for 2 minutes, or until light and fluffy. If the consistency appears too thick, add a teaspoon of milk and beat, but only if necessary. If the consistency appears too thin, add ¼ cup (29 g) of sifted confectioners' sugar. The frosting should be creamy and spreadable, but thick enough to hold its shape
4. Spread the frosting over the cooled cake and decorate with the nonpareils. Allow the frosting to set at room temperature for at least 20 minutes before serving.

Black Forest Cheesecake | YIELDS ONE 9-INCH CHEESECAKE

The only thing better than chocolate cheesecake? Chocolate cheesecake that's been spiked with Kirsch liqueur and topped with gooey cherry filling and freshly whipped cream! This recipe is heavenly and sure to impress.

CRUST

Nonstick baking spray

36 Oreo cookies (420 g), crushed into fine crumbs

6 tablespoons (85 g) unsalted butter, melted

CHOCOLATE CHEESECAKE

9 ounces (254 g) 70% dark chocolate, coarsely chopped

2 teaspoons espresso powder

24 ounces (680 g) full-fat cream cheese, room temperature

¼ cup (57 g) full-fat sour cream, room temperature

1 cup (198 g) granulated sugar

¼ cup (53 g) packed light brown sugar

4 large eggs plus 2 egg yolks, room temperature

¾ cup (170 ml) heavy cream, room temperature

2 tablespoons (28 ml) Kirsch liqueur

2 teaspoons pure vanilla extract

1 tablespoon (5 g) Dutch-process cocoa powder, sifted

CHERRY TOPPING

2½ cups (400 g) fresh or frozen cherries (if using frozen, don't thaw)

2½ tablespoons (35 ml) Kirsch liqueur

1 tablespoon (14 g) granulated sugar

2½ teaspoons cornstarch

FOR THE CRUST

1. Preheat the oven to 350°F. Lightly grease the bottom and sides of a 9-inch springform pan with nonstick baking spray. Wrap the bottom and sides of the pan well with several layers of extra-wide heavy-duty aluminum foil. (This is to ensure no water seeps in when the pan is in the water bath.)

2. In a large bowl, mix the cookie crumbs and melted butter together until well combined.

3. Press the cookie mixture into the prepared pan, pressing down firmly across the bottom and about ½ inch up the sides.

4. Bake the crust for 12 minutes. Place the partially baked crust on a wire rack and set it aside while you prepare the filling. Reduce the oven temperature to 325°F.

FOR THE CHEESECAKE

1. Fill a medium saucepan one-third full with water and bring it to a low simmer over moderate heat.

2. On top of the pan place a heatproof bowl that fits snugly without the bottom of the bowl touching the water. Reduce the heat to low and add the chocolate and espresso powder to the bowl. Heat until the chocolate is completely melted, stirring occasionally with a rubber spatula. Carefully remove the bowl from the pan and set it aside.

3. In the bowl of a food processor, or in a large bowl using a handheld electric mixer, beat the cream cheese and sour cream until completely smooth, scraping down the bowl as needed. Add both sugars and beat smooth.

4. On low speed, add the eggs and egg yolks, one at a time, beating just until combined. (Don't overmix; if too much air is incorporated into the batter, it will rise in the oven and fall as it cools.)

5. Add the heavy cream, Kirsch, and vanilla and beat on low speed just until combined, about 20 more seconds. Using a rubber spatula, fold in the melted chocolate and cocoa powder, mixing until evenly incorporated.

6. Remove the bowl from the food processor and, using a rubber spatula, stir the filling several times to ensure it's evenly blended.

7. Pour the filling on top of the partially baked crust and, using a rubber spatula, smooth the top.

continues on p. 138

WHIPPED CREAM

1½ cups (340 ml) heavy cream, cold

⅓ cup (38 g) confectioners' sugar sifted

4 ounces (113 g) 70% dark chocolate, coarsely grated into shavings

---

> **ASHLEY'S TIP**
>
> *If you can't find Kirsch liqueur, or prefer not to consume alcohol, an equal amount of cherry juice can be used in its place.*
>
> *The cheesecake will keep, covered in the refrigerator, for 5 days, or wrapped tightly and frozen, for 2 months. If freezing, thaw overnight in the refrigerator before slicing.*

8. Place the cheesecake into a large deep pan. Then fill the pan with 3 inches of hot water to create a water bath. (This helps ensure the cheesecake comes out crack-free.)

9. Carefully place the pan in the oven and bake for 1 hour and 10 minutes. Don't worry if the center of the cheesecake is still slightly wiggly; the cake will set completely as it cools.

10. Remove cheesecake from the oven and gently run a knife around the edge of the cake. Place the cheesecake pan on a wire rack and cool completely. Loosely cover the pan with plastic wrap and chill in the refrigerator for at least 8 hours, or up to 5 days. (Note: The cheesecake should be fully chilled before removing the springform pan.)

FOR THE TOPPING

1. In a medium saucepan, combine all the ingredients. Bring to a boil over medium-high heat, stirring almost constantly, then reduce to simmer and cook for 6 to 8 minutes, until the mixture starts to thicken.

2. Reduce the heat to low and cook for 2 more minutes before transferring the topping to a heatproof bowl. Cool completely then cover and chill in the refrigerator for at least 2 hours, and up to 24 hours. Stir well before using.

3. Right before serving, spread the topping evenly across the top of the chilled cheesecake. Top with the whipped cream and chocolate shavings and serve at once.

FOR THE WHIPPED CREAM

1. In the bowl of a stand mixer fitted with the whisk attachment, or in a large bowl using a handheld electric mixer, beat the cream on medium-low speed, slowly adding the confectioners' sugar.

2. Once all the sugar has been added, increase to medium-high speed and whip until medium-stiff peaks form.

3. Right before serving, pipe or dollop the whipped cream on top of the cake.

Sparkling Champagne Cupcakes | YIELDS 24 CUPCAKES

Nothing screams "Let's celebrate!" quite like Champagne. But cupcakes are almost equally as festive, and they are a staple at holiday parties far and wide. So what happens when you combine the two? You end up with the most celebratory dessert treat ever. Just a word to the wise: between the Champagne cupcakes, Champagne soaking syrup, and Champagne frosting, you can definitely taste the booze! They are probably best served to adults only.

CHAMPAGNE CUPCAKES

Nonstick baking spray

3⅓ cups (400 g) all-purpose flour

1 tablespoon (14 g) baking powder

½ teaspoon baking soda

½ teaspoon salt

2 sticks (227 g) unsalted butter, room temperature

1½ cups (298 g) granulated sugar

6 large egg whites, room temperature, lightly beaten until foamy

½ cup (113 g) full-fat sour cream, room temperature

¼ cup (57 ml) whole milk, room temperature

¼ cup (50 ml) vegetable oil

2 teaspoons pure vanilla extract

1 cup (227 ml) Champagne or prosecco

FOR THE CUPCAKES

1. Preheat the oven to 350°F. Line two regular 12-cup muffin tins with paper liners, grease lightly with nonstick baking spray. Set the pans aside.

2. In a large bowl, sift together the flour, baking powder, baking soda, and salt. Set the bowl aside.

3. In the bowl of a stand mixer fitted with the paddle attachment, or in a large bowl using a handheld electric mixer, beat the butter on medium speed, about 1 minute, until smooth and creamy.

4. Gradually add the sugar, beating until smooth after each addition, and scraping down the bottom and sides of the bowl as needed. Once all the sugar has been added, increase speed to medium-high and beat about 2 minutes, until light and fluffy. Turn the mixer off and scrape down the sides and bottom of the bowl, then beat on medium speed for 30 more seconds.

5. Reduce mixer speed to medium-low. Add the egg whites in three parts, beating well after each addition, and turning off the mixer and scraping down the sides and bottom of the bowl as needed.

6. In a large glass measuring cup with a spout, whisk together the sour cream, milk, oil, and vanilla until well combined.

7. With the mixer on the lowest speed, add the flour mixture in three additions, alternating with the sour cream mixture in two additions, beginning and ending with the flour mixture, and mixing until just combined.

8. Slowly pour in the Champagne and, using a rubber spatula, fold it into the batter until just combined.

9. Divide the cupcake batter evenly among the prepared pans. Bake, one tray at a time, for 16 to 18 minutes, or until the cupcakes are domed, slightly golden, and a toothpick inserted in the center comes out clean.

10. Transfer the pan to a wire rack and cool the cupcakes in the pan for 10 minutes. Then remove the cupcakes from the pan, place them on the wire rack, and brush with the soaking syrup.

ASHLEY'S TIP

No need to splurge on expensive Champagne for this recipe. A dry prosecco or cava will work just fine.

---

continues on p. 142

CHAMPAGNE SOAKING SYRUP

¼ cup (57 ml) water

¼ cup (50 g) granulated sugar

½ cup (113 ml) Champagne or prosecco

CHAMPAGNE FROSTING

8 ounces (227 g) full-fat cream cheese, room temperature

2 sticks (227 g) unsalted butter, room temperature

5 cups (570 g) confectioners' sugar, sifted, plus more as needed

3 tablespoons (42 ml) Champagne or prosecco, plus more as needed

¼ teaspoon salt

Champagne-colored food-grade sparkle dust or edible gold leaf, for garnish, (optional)

FOR THE SOAKING SYRUP

1. In a medium saucepan over medium heat, whisk together the water and sugar and cook until the sugar dissolves, then bring to a boil and continue cooking for 2 minutes, stirring frequently.

2. Remove the pan from the heat and stir in the Champagne. Pour the syrup into a heatproof bowl and set it aside to cool.

3. Using a thin skewer or toothpick, poke holes all over the top of the cupcakes. Using a pastry brush, gently brush the syrup on top of each cupcake, working slowly so the cakes absorb the syrup. There is enough syrup to do 3 or 4 coats on each cupcake.

4. Allow the cupcakes to cool completely before frosting.

FOR THE FROSTING

1. In the bowl of a stand mixer fitted with the paddle attachment, or in a large bowl using a handheld electric mixer, beat the cream cheese and butter on medium speed until smooth and creamy.

2. Reduce the speed to low and gradually add the confectioners' sugar, beating well after each addition. Add the Champagne and salt and beat until smooth. Increase the speed to medium-high and beat for 2 minutes, or until light and fluffy.

3. If the consistency appears too thick, add a teaspoon of Champagne and beat, but only if necessary. If the consistency appears too thin, add ¼ cup (29 g) of sifted confectioners' sugar. The frosting should be creamy and spreadable, but also thick enough to hold its shape when piped.

4. Scrape the frosting into a large piping bag fitted with an open star tip. Pipe generous swirls of frosting on top of each cooled cupcake, then sprinkle with sparkle dust or decorate with gold leaf, if desired.

Cranberry Cherry Pie | YIELDS ONE 9-INCH PIE

This recipe, like this book, is dedicated to my mom. She had a deep affection for cherry pie and was always not-so-subtly hinting I should bake one for our next get-together. Cherry pie is traditionally a summertime treat, but I made this version "holiday appropriate" by adding cranberries and using frozen cherries. It's not too sweet, perfectly juicy, and just begging to be served with a giant scoop of vanilla ice cream. This one is for you, Mom . . . and for all my cherry pie lovers out there!

CRUST

5 cups (600 g) all-purpose flour

¼ cup (50 g) granulated sugar

½ teaspoon salt

4 sticks (454 g) very cold unsalted butter, cut into ½-inch cubes

1 cup (227 ml) ice water (you may not use it all)

CRANBERRY CHERRY FILLING

3 cups (492 g) fresh or frozen cherries (if frozen, don't thaw)

3 tablespoons (42 ml) Kirsch liqueur

2 tablespoons (28 g) packed light brown sugar

2 tablespoons plus 3 teaspoons (28 g) cornstarch, divided

2 cups (198 g) cranberries, fresh or frozen (if frozen, don't thaw)

¾ cup (149 g) granulated sugar

¼ teaspoon almond extract

¼ teaspoon ground cinnamon

1 large egg

1½ teaspoons water

¼ cup (50 g) sparkling sugar

FOR THE CRUST

1. In a large bowl, mix together the flour, sugar, and salt. Add the butter and toss with a spatula to coat the butter in the flour.

2. Using a pastry cutter, work the butter into the flour until the mixture resembles a coarse meal. The bits of butter should be about the size of peas.

3. Using a rubber spatula, slowly blend in just enough ice water to form moist clumps, start with ¾ cup (170 ml) water.

4. Scrape the shaggy dough out onto a clean surface and knead it gently, until it comes together in a ball, adding more ice water only if absolutely needed. (Note: The less water you add, the flakier your crust will be. Try to knead it together without additional water and add a small amount only if absolutely needed.)

5. Gather the dough into a large ball and divide it in half (each half will weigh about 21 ounces/605 g, depending on how much water you use). Gently flatten each half into a disk.

6. Wrap the disks in plastic wrap and place in the refrigerator to chill for at least 2 hours, or up to 24 hours.

FOR THE FILLING

1. In a medium saucepan, combine the cherries, Kirsch, brown sugar, and 3 teaspoons (6 g) of the cornstarch. Place the pan over medium-high heat and bring to a boil, stirring almost constantly. Cook for 10 minutes, or until the mixture has thickened enough to coat the back of a spoon.

2. Reduce the heat to low and cook for 2 more minutes before removing from the heat.

3. Transfer the mixture to a large heatproof bowl and stir in the cranberries, sugar, almond extract, cinnamon, and the remaining cornstarch (22 g). Mix well to evenly combine, then set it aside to cool completely, about 1 hour.

PREPARE THE BOTTOM CRUST

1. Remove one disk of the dough from the fridge 15 minutes before you plan to roll it out (dough that is too cold will crack).

ASHLEY'S TIP

If the crust is getting too brown, add a pie crust shield or gently tent aluminum foil on top of the pie.

---

continues on p. 146

2. Lightly flour a rolling pin and a large clean work surface. Set the dough in the middle of the work surface and, starting from the center of the disk, roll the dough away from you in one firm and even stroke. After each stroke, rotate the disk a quarter turn clockwise and roll again. Lightly sprinkle more flour as needed. You want to use just enough to prevent the dough from sticking. As the disk of dough becomes larger, be sure not to overstretch the center of the dough. Continue rolling until the dough is 16 inches in diameter, and ¼-inch thick.

3. Carefully fold the dough in half and lay it across one side of a 9-inch pie pan, placing the seam of the dough in the center of the pan. (Note: I suggest using a metal or glass pie plate. Ceramic may take longer to bake and may yield a less flaky crust.)

4. Gently unfold the crust, then fit the dough down into the pan, ensuring there are no gaps between the dough and the sides of the pan. If you see any visible air bubbles, gently poke them with a fork.

5. Using kitchen scissors, trim the dough overhang to 1½ inches, measuring from the inner rim of the pan.

6. Lightly cover the crust with plastic wrap and refrigerate until needed.

PREPARE THE LATTICE CRUST

1. Remove the second disk of the dough from the fridge and let it sit at room temperature for 15 minutes before you plan to roll. Line a large baking sheet with parchment paper and set it aside.

2. Follow the instructions for rolling in step 2 for the bottom crust.

3. Using a pizza cutter or pastry roller, slice the dough into twelve 1-inch strips. Gently lay the strips on the prepared baking sheet, cover with plastic wrap, and refrigerate until needed.

TO ASSEMBLE AND BAKE

1. Position a rack in lower third of the oven. Preheat the oven to 425°F. Line a large baking sheet with parchment paper and set it aside.

2. Remove the bottom crust and lattice strips from the refrigerator.

3. Sprinkle the bottom of the pie crust with 1 teaspoon of flour. Then, using a rubber spatula, scrape the filling into the pie crust shell.

4. Lay 7 of the strips parallel on top of the filling, leaving about ⅛ inch between each strip. Fold back the second, fourth, and sixth strip, then place a strip of dough perpendicular to the parallel strips. Unfold the folded strips, so they lie over the perpendicular strip.

5. Now fold back the first, third, fifth, and seventh strip, then place another strip of dough on top, so that it's perpendicular to the parallel lattice strips. Repeat to complete weaving all the strips.

6. Trim the edges of the strips, leaving ½ inch of overhang. Tightly roll the excess dough up so it sits firmly on the edge of the pie plate, then crimp the edges to secure the strips with the bottom crust.

7. Whisk together the egg and water and gently brush the top and edges of the crust with the egg wash. Sprinkle generously with sparkling sugar.

8. Place the pie on the prepared baking sheet and bake for 18 minutes.

9. Reduce the oven temperature to 350°F and continue baking for 60 minutes, or until the top crust is golden brown and the filling is bubbling (see Tip).

10. Place the pie plate on a wire rack and cool for at least 4 hours before slicing.

11. Once the pie is completely cool, it may be wrapped tightly in plastic wrap and stored at room temperature for up to 48 hours.

Desserts

ASHLEY'S TIP

If you want to bake and freeze your cake layers in advance, follow the steps listed in my Tips section on page 128.

Gingerbread Celebration Cake | YIELDS ONE 9-INCH LAYER CAKE

There are few flavors in the world more festive than gingerbread! Aromatic and absolutely delicious—just thinking about it puts me in a good mood. And this cake is a full-blown gingerbread celebration. It features three layers of gingerbread cake, creamy mascarpone frosting, gooey cranberry filling, plus candied cranberries and rosemary sprigs. If you want a jaw-dropping holiday showstopper that will impress all your guests, this is it!

GINGERBREAD CAKE

Nonstick baking spray

2½ cups (300 g) all-purpose flour

2 tablespoons (10 g) Dutch-process cocoa powder, sifted

1 tablespoon (5 g) ground ginger

2 teaspoons baking powder

2 teaspoons ground cinnamon

1 teaspoon espresso powder

1 teaspoon ground allspice

½ teaspoon baking soda

½ teaspoon salt

½ teaspoon ground cloves

½ teaspoon ground nutmeg

¼ teaspoon ground cardamom

2 sticks (227 g) unsalted butter, melted

1½ cups (320 g) packed dark brown sugar

1 cup (340 ml) unsulphured molasses (not blackstrap)

½ cup (113 g) full-fat sour cream, room temperature

2 tablespoons (22 g) finely grated fresh ginger

1½ tablespoons (21 ml) vegetable oil

4 large eggs, room temperature

¾ cup (170 ml) boiling water

CRANBERRY FILLING

2 tablespoons (22 g) cornstarch

1½ tablespoons (21 ml) fresh orange juice

3 cups (298 g) fresh or frozen cranberries (if frozen, do not thaw)

1 cup (198 g) granulated sugar

⅔ cup (151 ml) water

¼ teaspoon salt

FOR THE CAKE

1. Preheat the oven to 350°F. Line the bottoms of three 9-inch cake pans with parchment paper rounds, then grease the pans and paper with nonstick baking spray. Set the pans aside.

2. In a medium bowl, whisk the flour, cocoa powder, ground ginger, baking powder, cinnamon, espresso powder, allspice, baking soda, salt, cloves, nutmeg, and cardamom together until well combined. Set it aside.

3. In a large bowl, whisk the melted butter, brown sugar, molasses, sour cream, fresh ginger, oil, and eggs together until well combined, about 2 minutes.

4. Using a rubber spatula, fold the flour mixture into the egg mixture, mixing until just combined. Pour in the hot water and whisk until just combined.

5. Divide the batter evenly (about 570 ml batter per pan) among the prepared baking pans. Bake, rotating the pans halfway through baking, for 18 to 20 minutes, or until a toothpick inserted in the center of a cake comes out clean.

6. Transfer the pans to wire racks and cool for 20 minutes. Then invert the cakes onto the racks to cool completely. (Note: The cakes do not rise much and bake up flat.)

FOR THE FILLING

1. In a small bowl, combine the cornstarch and orange juice. Whisk until completely blended. Set it aside.

2. In a medium saucepan, combine the cranberries, sugar, water, and salt. Bring to a simmer over medium heat, stirring occasionally, and cook for 5 minutes, or until the sugar has dissolved. Continue cooking, about 5 more minutes, until the cranberries soften and some have begun to burst.

3. Pour in the cornstarch mixture and mix well to combine. Continue cooking, about 5 more minutes, stirring constantly with a wooden spoon or rubber spatula, until the mixture has thickened.

4. Remove the pan from the heat and stir in the lemon juice and vanilla. Scrape into a bowl and cool completely before using, about 1 hour. (Note: Filling can be made up to 24 hours in advance and stored, covered, in the refrigerator. Bring to room temperature and stir well before using.)

continues on p. 150

1 tablespoon (14 ml) fresh lemon juice

1½ teaspoons pure vanilla extract

MASCARPONE FROSTING

3 sticks (340 g) unsalted butter, room temperature

8 ounces (227 g) mascarpone cheese, room temperature

4½ cups (513 g) confectioners' sugar, sifted

3½ tablespoons (49 ml) whole milk, plus more if needed

1 teaspoon pure vanilla extract

⅛ teaspoon salt

SUGARED CRANBERRIES AND ROSEMARY

2 cups (396 g) granulated sugar, divided

1 cup (227 ml) water

1½ cups (149 g) fresh cranberries

10 sprigs fresh rosemary (the thicker and fresher the better), trimmed to fit the pan

FOR THE FROSTING

1. In the bowl of a stand mixer fitted with the paddle attachment, or in a large bowl using a handheld electric mixer, beat the butter and mascarpone on medium speed until smooth and creamy, stopping the mixer occasionally to scrape down the sides and bottom of the bowl, about 2 minutes.

2. Reduce the mixer speed to low, and gradually add the confectioners' sugar, beating well after each addition. Add the milk, vanilla, and salt and beat until smooth.

3. Increase the mixer speed to medium-high and beat for 2 minutes, or until the frosting is light and fluffy. If it appears too stiff to spread, add more milk, a teaspoon at a time, until desired texture is achieved.

FOR THE CRANBERRIES AND ROSEMARY

1. In a medium saucepan, combine 1 cup (198 g) of the sugar and the water. Bring the mixture to a rolling boil over medium-high heat and cook, stirring frequently, until the sugar has completely dissolved.

2. Add the cranberries and bring the mixture back to a boil, then reduce the heat to a simmer and cook for 1 minute. Using a slotted spoon, remove the cranberries and transfer to a wire rack.

3. Add the rosemary to the simmering sugar mixture and cook for 1 minute, then use a slotted spoon to remove and transfer to the wire rack.

4. Allow the cranberries and rosemary to sit at room temperature for 10 minutes, or until still slightly sticky to the touch.

5. Add the remaining 1 cup (198 g) of sugar to a wide, shallow bowl. Add a few cranberries at a time, rolling them in the sugar until completely coated. Return the cranberries to the wire rack. Repeat with the rosemary sprigs.

6. Allow to dry at room temperature for at least 1 hour before using. (Note: Sparkling cranberries and rosemary can be made up to 48 hours in advance. Store them in the refrigerator, in an airtight container. If they lose any of their "sparkle", simply roll them in more sugar to freshen them up.)

TO ASSEMBLE

1. Carefully transfer one cake layer to a large plate or cake stand. Spread an even layer of frosting on top, about ¼-inch thick, then top with half of the cranberry filling. Repeat this process with another cake layer.

2. Top with the final cake layer and use the remaining frosting to cover the top and sides of the cake: ¼-inch thick on top, then spread whatever is left around the edges. This is a semi-naked cake, so it's okay if the sides aren't completely covered with frosting.

3. Decorate the cake with sugared cranberries and rosemary. Allow the cake to set at room temperature for at least 1 hour before slicing and serving.

6
CHAPTER

Cookies & Bars

The most wonderful time of year calls for cookies—and lots of them! So in this chapter you'll find recipes to keep your cookie jar full all season long. But there are also plenty of recipes for days you're looking to branch out *beyond* the cookie jar . . . from decadent brownies to gooey apple pie bars to classic butter cookies you can decorate a dozen different ways, there's truly something for everyone. Happy baking!

My Favorite Butter Cookies | 154

Triple Chocolate Brownies | 159

Oatmeal Chocolate Chunk Cookies | 160

Cranberry-Pistachio Biscotti | 163

Lemon White Chocolate Macadamia Nut Cookies | 167

Chocolate Crinkles | 168

Molasses Cream Pies | 171

Salted Caramel Apple Pie Bars | 173

Peanut Butter M&M® Cookies | 176

Brown Butter Blondies | 179

My Favorite Butter Cookies | YIELDS ABOUT 2 DOZEN COOKIES

One cookie a million different ways? Count me in! Okay . . . maybe not a million, but it's a pretty darn versatile dough. Use it to make cutout cookies shaped like Christmas trees, candy canes, stars, or snowflakes! Or use it to make slice & bake cookies, shortbread cookies, or thumbprints! Deciding what shapes and sizes you'll bake is only half the fun, because these buttery cookies are begging to be decorated. Dip them in chocolate, cover them in glaze, go crazy with colorful sprinkles, or stuff them with jam!

BUTTER COOKIES

2 sticks (227 g) unsalted butter, room temperature

1 cup (198 g) granulated sugar

1 large egg plus 2 egg yolks, room temperature

1 tablespoon (14 ml) pure vanilla extract

3 cups (360 g) all-purpose flour, plus more for dusting

¼ teaspoon salt

GLAZE

1 cup (113 g) confectioners' sugar, sifted

1½ tablespoons (21 ml) whole milk, plus more if needed

CHOCOLATE COATING

8 ounces (227 g) 70% dark chocolate, finely chopped

GARNISHES

Crushed candy canes

Chopped pistachios

Blue or silver sprinkles

Red and green nonpareils or sprinkles

Raspberry jam, or your favorite flavor

Nutella®

Confectioners' sugar

FOR CUTOUT BUTTER COOKIES

1. In the bowl of a stand mixer fitted with the paddle attachment, or in a large bowl using a handheld electric mixer, beat the butter and sugar on medium speed until combined, about 1 minute. Increase the speed to medium-high and continue beating for 2 minutes, until light and fluffy.

2. Reduce the speed to medium, then add the egg and egg yolks, beating until well combined, scraping down the sides and bottom of the bowl as needed. Beat in the vanilla.

3. On low speed, gradually add the flour and salt, and beat until combined. Your dough should be stiff.

4. Sprinkle a tablespoon (14 g) of flour over a clean work surface. Scrape the cookie dough onto the surface and gently knead it for 30 seconds. Divide the dough in half (about 445 g per half).

5. Press each portion of cookie dough into a 6-inch disk. Wrap dough tightly in plastic wrap and refrigerate for at least 3 hours (or up to 2 days).

6. When you're ready to bake, preheat the oven to 350°F. Line two large baking sheets with parchment paper.

7. Working with one disk at a time, unwrap the dough and transfer to a lightly floured surface. Using a rolling pin, roll the disk out to ¼-inch thickness.

8. Use decorative cookie cutters to cut out as many shapes as you can. Carefully transfer the shapes to the prepared baking sheet, leaving 1 inch between the cookies. Repeat with the remaining dough. Any dough scraps can be chilled and carefully rolled out again.

9. Bake for 10 to 12 minutes, or until lightly golden. Cool the cookies on the baking sheet for 15 minutes before transferring them to a wire rack to cool completely.

FOR THE GLAZE

1. In a wide shallow bowl, whisk together the confectioners' sugar and milk until well combined. The mixture should be thick but pourable.

2. Dip the top of a cooled cookie into the glaze, allowing excess glaze to drip back into the bowl before transferring it to a wire rack. Sprinkle with your favorite toppings. Repeat with as many cookies as desired.

3. Allow the glaze to set for at least 1 hour before serving.

continues on p. 156

FOR THE CHOCOLATE COATING

1. Fill a medium saucepan one-third full with water. Bring to a simmer over moderate heat. On top of the pan place a heatproof bowl that fits snugly without the bottom of the bowl touching the water. Reduce the heat to low. Place the chopped chocolate into the bowl and cook, stirring occasionally with a rubber spatula, until completely melted and smooth.

2. Dip a cookie halfway into the melted chocolate, allowing excess chocolate to drip back into the bowl before transferring it to a wire rack. You can also dip the top of a cookie fully in chocolate for a different look. Sprinkle with your favorite toppings. Repeat with as many cookies as desired.

3. Allow the chocolate to fully set before serving, about 1 hour.

VARIATIONS:

SLICE & BAKE COOKIES

1. At step 4, roll each portion of dough into a log 2 inches in diameter. Wrap the logs tightly in plastic wrap and refrigerate for at least 3 hours (or up to 2 days).

2. Use a sharp knife to slice the logs of cookie dough into ¼-inch rounds. Place the cookies ½ inch apart on the prepared baking sheets.

3. Bake for 10 to 12 minutes, or until lightly golden. Cool the cookies on the baking sheet for 15 minutes before transferring them to a wire rack to cool completely.

4. Dip half of each cookie in the chocolate coating or glaze and sprinkle with your favorite topping.

THUMBPRINT COOKIES

1. After making the dough, use a small spring-loaded measuring spoon to scoop out a heaping tablespoon (about 30 g) of dough. Roll it into a ball and place it on the prepared baking sheet. Use your thumb to make an indentation in the center of the dough. Repeat with all dough, leaving 2 inches between each cookie.

2. Bake for 12 minutes. Remove the cookies from the oven and fill each indentation with 1 teaspoon of jam, then bake for 6 more minutes, or until lightly golden.

3. Cool the cookies on the baking sheet, placed on top of a wire rack, for 1 hour before serving.

SANDWICH COOKIES

1. Follow instructions for cutout cookies, but roll the dough out slightly thinner, to ⅛-inch thickness. Use round or scalloped round cookie cutters to cut out an even number of rounds. Carefully transfer the rounds to the prepared baking sheet, leaving 1 inch between cookies.

2. Bake for 8 minutes, or until lightly golden. Cool the cookies on the baking sheet for 20 minutes before transferring them to a wire rack to cool completely.

3. Once cool, spread a cookie with a teaspoon or two of Nutella® or raspberry jam. Sandwich another cookie on top and lightly press together. Repeat with as many cookies as desired.

Cookies & Bars

Triple Chocolate Brownies | YIELDS ONE 9 X 13-INCH PAN

These brownies are so intensely chocolatey they should probably come with a warning label. Rich, fudgy, and loaded with chocolate flavor in every ... single ... bite ... they're definitely for chocolate lovers only! Delicious with vanilla ice cream or cold milk.

Nonstick baking spray

2 cups (240 g) all-purpose flour

1 cup (85 g) Dutch-process cocoa powder

2 teaspoons espresso powder

½ teaspoon baking powder

½ teaspoon salt

3 sticks (340 g) unsalted butter

⅓ cup (67 ml) vegetable oil

3½ ounces (100 g) 72% dark chocolate, finely chopped

2¾ cups (545 g) granulated sugar, divided

4 large eggs plus 2 egg yolks

1 tablespoon (14 ml) pure vanilla extract

12 ounces (340 g) semisweet chocolate chips

1. Preheat the oven to 350°F. Line a 9 x 13-inch baking pan with parchment paper. Grease lightly with nonstick baking spray and set it aside.
2. In a large bowl, whisk the flour, cocoa powder, espresso powder, baking powder, and salt together until well combined. Set the bowl aside.
3. Fill a medium saucepan one-third full with water. Bring to a simmer over moderate heat. On top of the pan place a heatproof bowl that fits snugly without the bottom of the bowl touching the water. Reduce heat to low.
4. Place the butter, oil, chocolate, and ¾ cup (149 g) of the sugar into the bowl and cook, stirring frequently, until the butter and chocolate are completely melted. Whisk until smooth and carefully remove the bowl from the heat.
5. In a separate large bowl, whisk the eggs and egg yolks, the remaining 2 cups (396 g) of sugar, and the vanilla together until well combined, about 45 seconds.
6. Gradually add the warm butter mixture to the egg mixture, whisking constantly until completely combined.
7. Add the dry ingredients and chocolate chips and, using a rubber spatula, slowly stir until just combined. Do not overmix! (This will give you cakey brownies.) Scrape the batter into the prepared pan and smooth the top.
8. Bake for 30 minutes, or until the edges are firm and the top is shiny and slightly cracked. (Note: If you're using a glass or ceramic baking pan, you might need to increase the baking time 5 to 10 minutes, as these materials take longer to conduct heat.)
9. Place the pan on a wire rack to cool for at least 2 hours before slicing.

ASHLEY'S TIP

Don't overbake! If you notice a little wiggle in the middle of your brownies when you're removing them from the oven, don't fret—this is totally normal and actually a good thing. The brownies will firm up a great deal as they cool.

Oatmeal Chocolate Chunk Cookies | YIELDS ABOUT 2 DOZEN COOKIES

Brown butter is nutty, fragrant, and the secret ingredient in these giant oatmeal chocolate chunk cookies. The dough is very easy to quickly whip up and doesn't require any chilling, making it a very good recipe any time a cookie craving strikes.

2½ cups (300 g) all-purpose flour
2 cups (178 g) old-fashioned oats
1 teaspoon baking soda
½ teaspoon ground cinnamon
½ teaspoon salt
2 sticks (227 g) unsalted butter
1½ cups (319 g) packed light brown sugar
½ cup (99 g) granulated sugar
1 tablespoon (14 ml) pure vanilla extract
2 large eggs plus 1 egg yolk, room temperature
12 ounces (340 g) 72% dark chocolate, chopped into rough chunks
2 teaspoons flaky sea salt

1. Preheat the oven to 350°F. Line two large baking sheets with parchment paper and set them aside.
2. In a medium bowl, combine the flour, oats, baking soda, cinnamon, and salt. Set the bowl aside.
3. In a large saucepan over medium heat, melt the butter. Continue cooking, swirling the pan occasionally, until the butter turns a golden-brown color, about 5 minutes. Remove the pan from the heat and scrape the butter, and any brown butter bits that have settled on the bottom of the pan, into a large bowl.
4. Whisk in both sugars and the vanilla, and beat well to combine, about 2 minutes. Whisk in the eggs and egg yolk, beating until fully incorporated into the batter.
5. Fold in the flour mixture and chocolate chunks, mixing just until everything is combined.
6. Using a large spring-loaded cookie scoop, scoop out about 3 tablespoons (80 g) of cookie dough and roll into a ball. Place the dough ball on the prepared baking sheet. Repeat with all cookie dough, leaving 2 inches between each cookie.
7. Bake, one sheet at a time, for 11 to 12 minutes, or until spread out and lightly golden brown in color.
8. Cool the cookies on the baking sheet for 20 minutes. Sprinkle with the sea salt and enjoy warm, or transfer to a wire rack to cool completely.

ASHLEY'S TIP

Not a chocolate chunk fan? You can omit the chocolate chunks and use an equal amount of chocolate chips, raisins, or even M&M's® in this recipe.

Cranberry-Pistachio Biscotti | YIELDS ABOUT 18 COOKIES

Ninety-nine percent of the time I want a cookie that's soft, chewy, and loaded with chocolate. But once in a while, I find myself craving crunchy cookies, and when I do, I bake biscotti. These twice-baked cookies are delightfully crisp, but not so hard you'll fear chipping a tooth. They're loaded with chewy cranberries and crunchy pistachios, plus just the right amount of festive spice. A great cookie to dip in your coffee or tea!

- 1 large egg
- 1 teaspoon water
- 2¼ cups (270 g) all-purpose flour, plus more for dusting
- 1½ teaspoons baking powder
- ½ teaspoon salt
- ½ teaspoon ground cinnamon
- ¼ teaspoon ground cardamom
- 6 tablespoons (85 g) unsalted butter, room temperature
- ¾ cup (149 g) granulated sugar
- ¼ cup (53 g) packed light brown sugar
- 2 large eggs plus 1 egg yolk, room temperature
- 1 tablespoon (14 ml) olive oil
- 2 teaspoons pure vanilla extract
- ¼ teaspoon almond extract
- 1 cup (113 g) lightly salted whole pistachios
- ¾ cup (85 g) dried cranberries (sweetened or unsweetened)
- ¼ cup (50 g) sparkling sugar
- 8 ounces (227 g) 70% dark chocolate, finely chopped
- ½ cup (57 g) lightly salted chopped pistachios

1. Preheat the oven to 350°F. Line a large baking sheet with parchment paper and set it aside.
2. In a small bowl, whisk together the egg and water until well combined. Set the bowl aside.
3. In a medium bowl, whisk together the flour, baking powder, salt, cinnamon, and cardamom. Set the bowl aside.
4. In the bowl of a stand mixer fitted with the paddle attachment, or in a large bowl using a handheld electric mixer, beat the butter and both sugars on medium speed for 2 minutes, scraping down the sides and bottom of the bowl as needed, until the mixture is combined but slightly crumbly.
5. Add the eggs and egg yolk, one at a time, beating well after each addition. Beat in the oil, vanilla, and almond extract.
6. On low speed, add the flour mixture and beat until just combined. Add in the whole pistachios and dried cranberries, mixing until just combined.
7. Scrape the dough out onto a lightly floured surface and, with lightly floured hands, gently knead the dough until it's soft and just slightly sticky, about 4 to 5 turns.
8. Divide the dough evenly in two pieces (about 16 ounces/425 g each) and place each half onto the prepared baking sheet, leaving at least 2 inches between the halves. Shape each half into a log about 9 inches long and 2 inches wide.
9. Using a pastry brush, lightly brush the top and sides of each slab with the egg wash. Then sprinkle with sparkling sugar.
10. Bake for 25 minutes, or until the top is lightly golden brown. Remove the pan from the oven, and reduce the oven temperature to 325°F.
11. Allow the biscotti to cool on the baking pan for exactly 10 minutes.
12. Carefully slice each slab into 1-inch slices. Place the slices, cut side up, back on the baking sheet, leaving ¼ inch between each biscotto.
13. Return the pan to the oven and bake for 8 minutes. Turn the biscotti over and bake for 8 more minutes, or until golden brown.
14. Cool the biscotti on the baking sheet for 15 minutes before transferring them to a wire rack to cool completely. (Note: keep the parchment paper lined baking sheets close by; you'll use them again in the next step.)

continues on p. 164

Cookies & Bars | 163

15. Make the chocolate coating. Fill a medium saucepan one-third full with water. Bring to a simmer over moderate heat. On top of the pan place a heatproof bowl that fits snugly without the bottom of the bowl touching the water. Reduce the heat to low.
16. Place the chopped chocolate into the bowl and cook, stirring occasionally with a rubber spatula, until completely melted.
17. Carefully remove the bowl from the pan, making sure no water comes in contact with the chocolate. Dip a biscotto into the melted chocolate. Then transfer it to the parchment lined baking sheet. Sprinkle with chopped pistachios. Repeat with all biscotti. Allow the chocolate to completely set before serving, about 1 hour.

Lemon White Chocolate Macadamia Nut Cookies | YIELDS ABOUT 2 DOZEN COOKIES

My love for white chocolate macadamia cookies was discovered, of all places, at Subway. Yes, the sandwich shop! I worked there as a teen (star sandwich maker right here!) and fell in love with them on my first shift. Soft, chewy, and loaded with creamy white chocolate and buttery macadamia nuts . . . what's not to love?! My version includes a pop of fresh lemon flavor, which provides a sunshiny sweetness that's always welcome on a cold winter's day.

3 cups (360 g) all-purpose flour

¾ teaspoon baking soda

½ teaspoon salt

2 sticks (227 g) unsalted butter, room temperature

1¼ cups (248 g) granulated sugar

¼ cup (53 g) packed light brown sugar

1 tablespoon (12 g) finely grated lemon zest

2 teaspoons pure vanilla extract

2 large eggs, room temperature

11 ounces (312 g) white chocolate chips, plus more for decorating

8 ounces (227 g) roasted macadamia nuts, plus more for decorating

1 tablespoon (14 g) flaky sea salt (optional)

1. Preheat the oven to 325°F. Line two large baking sheets with parchment paper and set them aside.

2. In a large bowl, whisk together the flour, baking soda, and salt. Set it aside.

3. In the bowl of a stand mixer fitted with the paddle attachment, or in a large bowl using a handheld electric mixer, combine the butter and both sugars and beat on medium speed for about 3 minutes, until light and fluffy, scraping down the bottom and sides of the bowl as needed. Beat in the lemon zest and vanilla.

4. Reduce the mixer speed to medium-low and beat in the eggs, one at a time, beating well after each addition, and scraping down the sides and bottom of the bowl as needed.

5. Reduce the mixer speed to low and add the flour mixture, beating until just combined. Add the white chocolate chips and macadamia nuts, mixing just until evenly combined.

6. Using a large spring-loaded cookie scoop, scoop about 3 tablespoons (75 g) of cookie dough and roll into a ball. Place the dough ball on the prepared sheet. Repeat with all dough, leaving 2 inches between each cookie.

7. Bake one sheet at a time for 11 to 12 minutes, or until golden at the edges but still soft in the middle.

8. Remove the cookies from the oven and, using a spatula, carefully tuck in any edges that may have spread too much while baking. Gently press extra white chocolate chips and macadamia nuts on top of the cookies and sprinkle with the sea salt, if using.

9. Cool the cookies on the baking sheet for 15 minutes before serving warm, or transferring to a wire rack to cool completely.

Chocolate Crinkles | YIELDS ABOUT 3 DOZEN COOKIES

Say hello to the most tested recipe in this entire book: I tested this recipe 27 times before finally getting it right ... and then five more times to ensure consistency. Was it worth it? Heck yes! These crinkly cookies are visually stunning and taste like a chewy brownie in cookie form. My favorite cookie to enjoy with a cold glass of milk.

- 7 ounces (200 g) 72% dark chocolate, finely chopped
- 1 stick (113 g) unsalted butter, cut into tiny cubes
- ¼ cup (50 ml) vegetable oil
- 1½ teaspoons espresso powder
- 2 cups (240 g) all-purpose flour
- ⅓ cup (28 g) Dutch-process cocoa powder
- 2 teaspoons baking powder
- ½ teaspoon salt
- 2 cups (396 g) granulated sugar, divided
- ½ cup (106 g) packed light brown sugar
- 3 large eggs plus 2 egg yolks, room temperature
- ¼ cup (57 g) full-fat sour cream, room temperature
- 1 tablespoon (14 ml) pure vanilla extract
- 1 cup (170 g) semisweet chocolate chips
- Nonstick baking spray
- 1 cup (114 g) confectioners' sugar

1. Fill a medium saucepan one-third full with water. Bring to a simmer over moderate heat. On top of the pan place a heatproof bowl that fits snugly without the bottom of the bowl touching the water. Reduce the heat to low.
2. Place the chocolate, butter, oil, and espresso powder into the bowl and cook, stirring occasionally, until the chocolate and butter are completely melted. Whisk until smooth and carefully remove the bowl from heat. Set it aside.
3. In a medium bowl, whisk the flour, cocoa powder, baking powder, and salt together until well combined. Set the bowl aside.
4. In a large bowl, whisk 1 cup (198 g) of the granulated sugar, the brown sugar, eggs and egg yolks, sour cream, and vanilla until well combined, about 30 seconds.
5. Gradually add the melted chocolate mixture into the egg mixture, whisking constantly. Fold in the flour mixture and chocolate chips, mixing just until just combined.
6. Cover and refrigerate for at least 2 hours or up to 24 hours.

WHEN READY TO BAKE

1. Preheat the oven to 325°F. Line two large baking sheets with parchment paper. Lightly grease the parchment paper with nonstick baking spray. Set them aside.
2. Place the remaining 1 cup (198g) of granulated sugar into a wide shallow bowl. Sift the confectioners' sugar into a separate wide shallow bowl.
3. Using a small spring-loaded cookie scoop, scoop out about 2 tablespoons (35 g) of cookie dough and roll it into a ball. Roll the ball in the granulated sugar first, then roll in the confectioners' sugar, ensuring the ball is well coated. Place the dough ball on the prepared baking sheet. Repeat with all dough, leaving 2 inches in between each cookie.
4. Bake, one sheet at a time, for 15 minutes, or until cookies have puffed up and the tops have begun to crack. Cool the cookies on the baking sheet, placed on top of a wire rack, for 30 minutes before serving.

ASHLEY'S TIP

Love chocolate and peppermint? Turn these into chocolate peppermint crinkles by adding some peppermint extract in step 4. Start with a ½ teaspoon, then work your way up to a full teaspoon if you want more peppermint flavor.

Molasses Cream Pies | YIELDS ABOUT 2 DOZEN CREAM PIES

This recipe was inspired by Little Debbie Oatmeal Creme Pies. Remember those? I used to love them . . . so much so that I decided to create a semi-sophisticated version that's perfect for the holidays. Here's what I came up with: chewy, aromatic molasses cookies stuffed with cream cheese frosting and swirled with a tiny dollop of vibrant orange marmalade. Flavorful, fun to eat, and totally festive. Nailed it!

MOLASSES COOKIES

5¾ cups (690 g) all-purpose flour

1 tablespoon (5 g) Dutch-process cocoa powder, sifted

1 tablespoon (14 g) baking soda

1 teaspoon baking powder

2 tablespoons (10 g) ground ginger

2½ teaspoons ground cinnamon

1 teaspoon ground cloves

¾ teaspoon ground allspice

½ teaspoon ground cardamom

½ teaspoon salt

¼ teaspoon finely ground black pepper

3 sticks (340 g) unsalted butter, room temperature

2¼ cups (479 g) packed light brown sugar

1 tablespoon (14 ml) pure vanilla extract

1 teaspoon finely grated orange zest

2 large eggs, room temperature

⅔ cup (227 g) unsulphured molasses (not blackstrap)

2 cups (397 g) sparkling sugar

FOR THE COOKIES

1. In a large bowl, whisk the flour, cocoa powder, baking soda, baking powder, ginger, cinnamon, cloves, allspice, cardamom, salt, and pepper together until well combined. Set the bowl aside.

2. In the bowl of a stand mixer fitted with the paddle attachment, or in a large bowl using a handheld electric mixer, beat together the butter and brown sugar on low speed until combined, then increase the speed to medium-high and continue beating about 2 to 3 minutes, until the mixture is light and fluffy, scraping down the sides and bottom of the bowl with a rubber spatula as needed.

3. Add the vanilla and orange zest and beat until combined.

4. Reduce the mixer speed to medium-low. Add the eggs, one at a time, beating well after each addition, and scraping the sides and bottom of the bowl as needed to incorporate. Add the molasses and beat until combined.

5. With the mixer on low, slowly add the flour mixture, beating only until everything is evenly incorporated, and scraping the bottom of the bowl as needed.

6. Cover the bowl and refrigerate for at least 4 hours, or up to 2 days.

WHEN READY TO BAKE

1. Preheat the oven to 350°F. Line two large baking sheets with parchment paper. Fill a wide, shallow bowl with sparkling sugar.

2. Using a medium spring-loaded cookie scoop, scoop out about 2 tablespoons (50 g) of cookie dough and roll it into a ball. Roll the ball in the sugar, ensuring the ball is well coated. Place the dough ball on the prepared baking sheet. Repeat with all dough, leaving 2 inches between each cookie.

3. Bake, one sheet at a time, for 12 minutes, or until the cookies have puffed up and have begun to slightly crack on top. (They will crack more as they cool, so don't overbake!)

4. Cool the cookies on the baking sheet for 15 minutes before transferring to a wire rack to cool completely. Then turn the cookies over so they are ready to be filled.

continues on p. 172

CREAM CHEESE FROSTING

8 ounces (227 g) full-fat cream cheese, room temperature

4 tablespoons (57 g) unsalted butter, room temperature

3½ cups (396 g) confectioners' sugar, sifted

1 tablespoon (14 ml) whole milk

1 teaspoon pure vanilla extract

⅛ teaspoon salt

½ cup (170 g) orange marmalade (I like Bonne Maman®)

FOR THE FROSTING

1. In the bowl of a stand mixer fitted with the paddle attachment, or in a large bowl using a handheld electric mixer, beat the cream cheese and butter on medium speed until completely smooth.

2. Reduce the speed to low and gradually add the confectioners' sugar, beating well after each addition. Add the milk, vanilla, and salt, and beat until smooth. Increase the speed to medium-high and beat for a minute, or until very fluffy.

3. Scrape the frosting into a large piping bag fitted with a large open round piping tip. Onto the bottom side of one cookie, pipe a swirl of frosting in the center of the cookie, leaving a ¼-inch border around the edges. Then top with 1 teaspoon of orange marmalade. Place another cookie on top and lightly press to seal them together. Repeat with all cookies.

4. Serve right away, or store in an airtight container in the refrigerator for up to 3 days. Bring to room temperature before serving.

Salted Caramel Apple Pie Bars | YIELDS ONE 9 X 13-INCH PAN

These bars will never be apple pie—but they're pretty darn close. (And so much easier to make!) These are especially great if you're serving a crowd. Featuring a buttery shortbread crust, tons of gooey apples, oatmeal crisp topping, and salted caramel, they're pretty much irresistible . . . especially if there's vanilla ice cream involved!

SHORTBREAD CRUST

Nonstick baking spray

3 sticks (340 g) unsalted butter, room temperature

½ cup (99 g) granulated sugar

3¾ cups (450 g) all-purpose flour

APPLE FILLING

8 large (1 kg) apples, peeled, cored, and thinly cut into ¼-inch slices

2 teaspoons fresh lemon juice

½ cup (99 g) granulated sugar

3 tablespoons (21 g) all-purpose flour

2 teaspoons ground cinnamon

½ teaspoon ground nutmeg

¼ teaspoon allspice

¼ teaspoon salt

OATMEAL CRISP TOPPING

1½ cups (134 g) old-fashioned oats

1 cup (120 g) all-purpose flour

¾ cup (149 g) granulated sugar

¾ cup (159 g) packed light brown sugar

1 teaspoon ground cinnamon

¼ teaspoon salt

2 sticks (227 g) unsalted butter, cut into ½-inch cubes, room temperature

FOR THE CRUST

1. Preheat the oven to 350°F. Line a 9 x 13-inch baking pan with parchment paper, allowing paper to overhang on two of the ends. Grease the parchment with nonstick baking spray. Set the pan aside.
2. In the bowl of a stand mixer fitted with the paddle attachment, or in a large bowl using a handheld electric mixer, beat together the butter and sugar for 2 to 3 minutes, until light and fluffy.
3. Reduce the speed to low, add the flour, and mix just until combined. The dough will be crumbly.
4. Press the dough evenly into the bottom of the prepared pan. Bake for 20 minutes.
5. Remove the pan from the oven and set it on a wire rack to cool. Keep the oven temperature at 350°F.

FOR THE FILLING

1. In a large bowl, combine the apples and lemon juice and toss to coat. Add the sugar, flour, cinnamon, nutmeg, allspice, and salt. Toss until the apples are evenly coated.
2. Arrange the apples in an even layer on top of the crust.

FOR THE TOPPING

1. In a large bowl, combine the oats, flour, both sugars, cinnamon, and salt. Add the cubed butter and, using a pastry blender, cut the butter into the dry ingredients until the mixture resembles a coarse meal. Sprinkle the topping evenly over the apples.
2. Bake the bars for 55 to 60 minutes, or until the top is golden brown and the apples are bubbling.
3. Transfer the pan to a wire rack and cool the bars for at least 2 hours in the pan before removing and slicing. The longer you cool, the neater your slices will be.

continues on p. 174

SALTED CARAMEL SAUCE

1 cup (198 g) granulated sugar

½ cup (113 ml) water

1 stick (113 g) unsalted butter

½ cup (113 ml) heavy cream

1½ teaspoons pure vanilla extract

1 teaspoon flaky sea salt, plus more for sprinkling (if desired)

FOR THE SAUCE

1. Whisk together the sugar and water in a medium saucepan with tall sides.
2. Cook over medium-low heat until the sugar is completely dissolved, 3 to 5 minutes (or longer depending on your stove).
3. Add the butter and bring the mixture to a slow boil over medium heat. Continue cooking without stirring until the mixture turns a deep golden brown-copper color, about 12 minutes (or until desired color is reached).
4. Once the caramel reaches this color, remove it from the heat and immediately add the cream. Take care doing this step; the caramel will hiss and bubble up aggressively.
5. Stir in the vanilla and salt. Vigorously whisk the mixture smooth and set it aside to cool.
6. Drizzle the sauce on top of the bars, sprinkle with additional sea salt, if desired, and serve.

Peanut Butter M&M® Cookies | YIELDS ABOUT 2 DOZEN COOKIES

I don't know if I'll ever love peanut butter, but over the last few years I've come to really like it. In fact, I even crave it sometimes. Specifically, in the form of these cookies. They have just the right amount of peanut butter flavor and they're packed with goodies like M&M's®, peanut butter chips, and gooey chocolate chips!

2⅓ cups (280 g) all-purpose flour

2 teaspoons baking powder

¾ teaspoon baking soda

½ teaspoon salt

⅛ teaspoon ground cinnamon

2 sticks (227 g) unsalted butter, room temperature

1 cup (269 g) creamy peanut butter

1 cup (198 g) granulated sugar

¾ cup (142 g) packed dark brown sugar

2 large eggs plus 1 egg yolk, room temperature

1 tablespoon (14 ml) pure vanilla extract

1½ cups (255 g) red and green M&M's®, plus more for decorating

1 cup (170 g) semisweet chocolate chips, plus more for decorating

1 cup (170 g) peanut butter chips

Flaky sea salt, for sprinkling (optional)

1. In a large bowl, whisk together the flour, baking powder, baking soda, salt, and cinnamon. Set the bowl aside.
2. In the bowl of a stand mixer fitted with the paddle attachment, or in a large bowl using a handheld electric mixer, beat the butter on medium speed until smooth. Add the peanut butter and beat until evenly combined.
3. Gradually add both sugars, one at a time, beating about 2 minutes until well combined. On low speed, add the eggs and egg yolk, one at a time, beating well after each addition, and scraping the sides and bottom of the bowl as needed. Beat in the vanilla.
4. Gradually add the dry ingredients, beating on low speed until just combined.
5. Using a rubber spatula, fold in the M&M's®, chocolate chips, and peanut butter chips.
6. Cover and refrigerate for at least 1 hour, or up to 48 hours.
7. About 30 minutes before you plan on baking, preheat the oven to 350°F. Line two large baking sheets with parchment paper. Set the pans aside.
8. Using a large spring-loaded cookie scoop, scoop about 3 tablespoons (80 g) of cookie dough and roll into a ball. Place the dough ball on the prepared baking sheet, leaving 2 inches between each cookie. Gently press down on each ball to flatten slightly. (This will help them spread evenly in the oven.)
9. Bake the cookies, one tray at a time, for 11 to 12 minutes, or until puffed up and slightly golden brown. Repeat with all the cookie dough.
10. When the cookies come out of the oven, decorate with a few extra chocolate chips and M&M's®. (This is best done while they're still warm!) Sprinkle with sea salt, if using.
11. Cool for at least 30 minutes on the baking sheet before serving, or transfer to a wire rack to cool completely.

ASHLEY'S TIP

If you can't find red and green M&M's®, or don't celebrate Christmas, use any color you desire.

Brown Butter Blondies | YIELDS ONE 9 X 13-INCH PAN

Blondies are the lazy baker's solution to making cookies for a crowd—no cookie dough chilling or rolling required! If you've never had a blondie before, I want to note that they are neither cookie bars nor brownies. They have a crunchy, cookie-like exterior, but remain slightly chewy and almost fudgy in the center, like a brownie. They are also infinitely adaptable! My favorite combination is brown butter, chocolate chips, and crunchy pecans, but if you don't care for that combo, you can toss in an equal amount of M&M's®, walnuts, dried cranberries, toffee bits, or pistachios instead!

- 3 sticks (340 g) unsalted butter
- 2 cups (425 g) packed light brown sugar
- ½ cup (99 g) granulated sugar
- 1 tablespoon (14 ml) pure vanilla extract
- 3 large eggs plus 1 egg yolk, room temperature
- 3⅓ cups (400 g) all-purpose flour
- ½ teaspoon baking powder
- ½ teaspoon salt
- 2 cups (340 g) semisweet chocolate chips, plus more for decorating
- 1 cup (110 g) pecans, roughly chopped, plus more for decorating
- 1 teaspoon flaky sea salt

1. Preheat the oven to 325°F. Line a 9 x 13-inch baking pan with parchment paper. Set it aside.
2. In a large saucepan over medium heat, melt the butter. Continue cooking, swirling the pan occasionally, until browned, about 5 minutes. Remove the pan from the heat and scrape the butter, and any brown butter bits that have settled on the bottom of the pan, into a large bowl.
3. Whisk in both sugars and mix until well combined. Whisk in the vanilla. Then add the eggs and egg yolk, one at a time, beating until well combined.
4. Using a rubber spatula, fold in the flour, baking powder, and salt, mixing until just combined. Fold in the chocolate chips and pecans.
5. Scrape the batter into the prepared pan and smooth as evenly as possible (the batter will be thick).
6. Bake for 35 to 36 minutes, or until the edges are firm and golden and the center is just slightly wobbly.
7. To garnish, press extra chocolate chips and pecans on top of the blondies as soon as they come out of the oven. Sprinkle with the sea salt.
8. Transfer the pan to a wire rack and cool for at least 2 hours before unmolding and cutting.

7
CHAPTER

Candy

This is the chapter where I convince you to make more homemade gifts this year. And by gifts, I mean, *candy*! To me, nothing says "I love you" or "I'm so glad we're friends" or "You're special to me" like a box of homemade truffles or peppermint bark. And since sharing is caring, you'll find all my favorite candy, chocolate, and caramel recipes here! Perfect for gifting during this magical season, even if it's just a gift to yourself. Because you're worth it!

Cherry-Almond Chocolate Bark | 182

Bourbon Butter Pecan Fudge | 185

Chocolate-Covered Peanut Butter Christmas Trees | 186

Kahlúa Peppermint Mocha Chocolate Truffles | 190

Dark Chocolate & Sea Salt Caramels | 193

Chocolate-Covered Almond Toffee | 197

Coconut-Pecan Truffles | 198

Peppermint Bark | 201

Cherry-Almond Chocolate Bark | YIELDS ONE 9 X 9-INCH PAN

It really doesn't get easier than chocolate bark. So, if you're a candy novice, this is a great recipe to start with: It's essentially foolproof. But don't let its simplicity fool you . . . because this dark chocolate bark is a total superstar. Loaded with chewy cherries, sweet cinnamon, crunchy almonds, and a sprinkle of sea salt, it's sure to impress!

18 ounces (511 g) 70% dark chocolate, finely chopped

½ teaspoon ground cinnamon

1 cup (142 g) whole roasted unsalted almonds

¾ cup (106 g) dried cherries

1 teaspoon flaky sea salt

1. Line a 9 x 9-inch pan with parchment paper, allowing the paper to overhang on two of the sides. Set the pan aside.

2. Fill a medium saucepan one-third full with water and bring to a simmer over moderate heat. On top of the pan place a heatproof bowl that fits snugly without the bottom of the bowl touching the water. Reduce the heat to low. Place the chocolate and cinnamon into the bowl and cook, stirring occasionally with a rubber spatula, until completely melted.

3. Carefully remove the bowl from the pan, making sure no water comes in contact with the chocolate.

4. Pour the melted chocolate into the prepared baking pan. Sprinkle the wet chocolate with the almonds and cherries. Set the chocolate aside for 30 minutes, then sprinkle with the sea salt.

5. Set aside for 3 hours, or until very firm. Using a large, sharp knife, cut the bark into 3-inch pieces and serve at room temperature.

6. Store in an airtight container, in the refrigerator, or in a cool, dry place, for up to one week.

ASHLEY'S TIP

This recipe is very adaptable. So, if you're not a fan of dark chocolate, feel free to experiment with semisweet chocolate, or even white chocolate. Not a fan of dried cherries? Use dried cranberries instead. Hate almonds? Toss in some pistachios. Experiment to create something you love!

Bourbon Butter Pecan Fudge | YIELDS ONE 8 X 8-INCH PAN

Butter pecan is my favorite ice cream flavor, so it should come as no surprise that it also is my favorite flavor when it comes to fudge! The base of this fudge is white chocolate, which, on its own, doesn't have much flavor. But when you add brown butter, toasted pecans, a splash of bourbon, and cinnamon, something very special happens. This fudge is a flavor explosion, with a delightful crunch in every bite!

BUTTERED PECANS

1½ tablespoons (21 g) unsalted butter

1½ cups (170 g) pecan halves, roughly chopped

FUDGE

Nonstick baking spray

2 tablespoons (28 g) unsalted butter

20 ounces (568 g) good-quality white chocolate, roughly chopped

14 ounces (397 ml) sweetened condensed milk (not evaporated milk)

1½ tablespoons (21 ml) bourbon

1 teaspoon pure vanilla extract

¾ teaspoon ground cinnamon

¼ teaspoon salt

Flaky sea salt, for garnish (optional)

FOR THE PECANS

1. Melt butter in a large skillet over medium-low heat. Add the pecans and cook, stirring frequently, for 4 to 5 minutes, or until lightly toasted.
2. Using a large slotted spoon, transfer pecans to a clean plate and set them aside.

FOR THE FUDGE

1. Line an 8 x 8-inch baking pan with parchment paper, allowing paper to overhang on two of the sides. Grease the parchment and any exposed pan with nonstick baking spray and set the pan aside.
2. Melt the butter in a small saucepan over medium heat. Continue cooking, swirling the pan frequently, until browned, about 3 minutes. Don't walk away during this step; the butter can burn in a matter of seconds. Remove the pan from the heat and scrape the browned butter into a small bowl. Set it aside.
3. Fill a medium saucepan one-third full with water and bring to a simmer over moderate heat. On top of the pan place a heatproof bowl that fits snugly without the bottom of the bowl touching the water.
4. Reduce the heat to low and add the white chocolate, condensed milk, and browned butter to the bowl. Heat until the chocolate is completely melted, stirring occasionally with a rubber spatula.
5. Once the chocolate is completely melted, vigorously whisk the mixture until it is smooth, then carefully remove the bowl from the heat. Whisk in the bourbon, vanilla, cinnamon, and salt. Using a rubber spatula, fold in the buttered pecans.
6. Scrape the fudge into the prepared pan and smooth the top. Sprinkle with sea salt, if using. Refrigerate for at least 4 hours.
7. Gently run a butter knife around the edge of the pan to loosen the fudge. Remove the fudge and transfer it to a cutting board. Peel off the parchment paper, then slice the fudge into small pieces.
8. Store in an airtight container in the refrigerator, for up to 1 month. You can also freeze the fudge, in an airtight freezer-safe container, for up to 2 months.

> **ASHLEY'S TIP**
>
> *Sweetened condensed milk is not the same thing as evaporated milk. So be sure the container you grab says "sweetened condensed milk" on the front; otherwise the fudge won't set properly.*

Chocolate-Covered Peanut Butter Christmas Trees | YIELDS ABOUT 16 TREES

Are these not the cutest? Inspired by the Christmas tree–shaped peanut butter candies my mom used to put in my stocking, these homemade treats feature a sweet peanut butter filling and a crunchy chocolate coating! To make them even more fun, sprinkle on some festive colored nonpareils.

PEANUT BUTTER TREES

- 16 ounces (454 g) creamy peanut butter (Jif® is my brand of choice)
- 3 cups (342 g) confectioners' sugar, sifted, plus more if needed
- 4 tablespoons (57 g) unsalted butter, room temperature
- 1 teaspoon pure vanilla extract
- ¼ teaspoon fine sea salt
- 3 tablespoons (42 ml) whole milk

FOR THE TREES

1. Line an 8 x 8-inch baking pan with parchment paper, allowing paper to overhang on two of the sides. Set the pan aside.

2. In the bowl of a stand mixer fitted with the whisk attachment, or in a large bowl using a handheld electric mixer, combine the peanut butter, confectioners' sugar, butter, vanilla, and salt. Beat on medium-low speed until well combined, scraping the sides and bottom of the bowl as needed.

3. Add the milk, 1 tablespoon (14 ml) at a time, until it becomes a nice workable dough. (It should be a little sticky, but scoopable and easy to work with; the texture should be similar to Play-Doh®.) If it's too sticky, add more confectioners' sugar, 1 tablespoon (7 g) at a time, until desired consistency is reached. If it's too dry, add more milk, 1 teaspoon at a time.

4. Press the peanut butter mixture into the prepared baking pan. Place a sheet of plastic wrap over the surface, then gently press with your hands until it's evenly spread across the bottom of the pan. Place the pan in the freezer and chill for exactly 90 minutes.

5. In the meantime, line a large baking sheet with parchment paper and set it aside.

6. When the 90 minutes are up, remove the pan from the freezer. Use the parchment paper handles to lift the peanut butter mixture from the pan.

7. Using a 2-inch Christmas tree cookie cutter, cut out as many trees as you can. Gather the scraps, gently knead them into a ball, and press back into a flat surface to cut additional trees.

8. Carefully transfer the trees to the prepared baking sheet, then place in the freezer for 90 more minutes, or until completely firm. (Note: Because peanut butter softens very quickly, I suggest removing the trees from the freezer in batches to prevent them getting too soft while you're dipping.)

9. About 25 minutes before the trees are done chilling, make the chocolate coating.

ASHLEY'S TIP

If you don't have a Christmas tree cookie cutter, or don't celebrate Christmas, try using a small cookie cutter shaped like a heart, star, circle, or snowflake—almost any shape will do! The key is to ensure the cookie cutter isn't too big, I recommend something around 2 inches.

---

continues on p. 189

CHOCOLATE COATING

24 ounces (681 g) 70% dark chocolate, finely chopped

Red and green nonpareils (optional)

FOR THE COATING

1. Fill a medium saucepan one-third full with water and bring to a simmer over moderate heat. On top of the pan place a heatproof bowl that fits snugly without the bottom of the bowl touching the water. Reduce the heat to low and place two-thirds of the chocolate into the bowl. Place a candy thermometer into the chocolate and let it melt, stirring frequently, with a rubber spatula. *Do not let the temperature of the chocolate exceed 120°F.*

2. Once the chocolate has fully melted, carefully remove the bowl from the heat, but keep the pot of simmering water on the burner. Wipe the bottom of the bowl to remove any condensation.

3. Stir in the remaining chocolate, a little bit at a time, allowing what you've added to completely melt before adding more.

4. Set chocolate aside and allow it to cool to 84°F. Once the chocolate has reached this temperature, reheat it briefly by placing the bowl back over the simmering water for about 10 seconds, or until it's between 89° and 91°F. *Do not let the temperature of the chocolate exceed 91°F.*

5. Remove the bowl from the heat once you have reached the correct temperature. The chocolate should be smooth and glossy, with no streaks.

6. Using a fork or candy dipper, dip each tree into the chocolate, then lift it up over the bowl, allowing excess chocolate to drip back into the bowl before dunking it back in again, then lifting it out and allowing excess to drip into the bowl. Once the tree has been double dunked, carefully transfer it back to the prepared baking sheet. Note: To temper properly chocolate needs to stay at its working temperature (for this recipe, that's between 89° and 91°F). If the chocolate falls below that temperature while you're dipping, pause and briefly reheat it to the working temperature.

7. Drizzle small lines of chocolate on top of each tree, if desired. Sprinkle the top of each tree with nonpareils, if desired.

8. Set trees aside and allow the chocolate to set before serving, about 1 hour.

9. Store in an airtight container, at room temperature, for up to 1 week.

Kahlúa Peppermint Mocha Chocolate Truffles | YIELDS ABOUT 2 DOZEN TRUFFLES

Chocolate truffles are pretty darn great—so how do you make them even better? Well, if you have similar taste buds to me, it's by adding festive ingredients like peppermint, mocha, and Kahlúa! These are definitely a labor of love, but so worth it.

PEPPERMINT TRUFFLES

16 ounces (454 g) 70% dark chocolate, finely chopped

1 cup (227 ml) heavy cream

1 teaspoon espresso powder

6 tablespoons (85 g) unsalted butter, cut into ¼-inch cubes, room temperature

3 tablespoons (42 ml) Kahlúa liqueur

1¼ teaspoons peppermint extract

CHOCOLATE COATING

24 ounces (681 g) 70% dark chocolate, finely chopped

½ cup (88 g) peppermint candies, finely crushed

FOR THE TRUFFLES

1. Place the chocolate in a medium heatproof bowl. Set it aside.
2. In a small saucepan over medium heat, bring the cream to a boil. As soon as it begins to boil, remove the cream from the heat. Whisk in the espresso powder.
3. Pour the hot cream over the chocolate and allow the mixture to sit, untouched, for 1 minute. Then whisk until smooth. Stir in the butter, Kahlúa, and peppermint extract and vigorously whisk until smooth and shiny.
4. Set the bowl aside and cool the chocolate mixture to room temperature. Then tightly cover the bowl with plastic wrap and refrigerate for 3 hours or until firm enough to scoop.

FOR THE COATING

1. Fill a medium saucepan one-third full with water and bring to a simmer over moderate heat. On top of the pan place a heatproof bowl that fits snugly without the bottom of the bowl touching the water. Reduce the heat to low.
2. Place two-thirds of the chocolate into the bowl. Place a candy thermometer into the chocolate and let it melt, stirring frequently with a rubber spatula. *Do not let the temperature of the chocolate exceed 120°F.*
3. Once the chocolate has fully melted, carefully remove the bowl from the heat, but keep the pot of simmering water on the burner. Wipe the bottom of the bowl to remove any condensation.
4. Stir in the remaining chocolate, a little bit at a time, allowing what you've added to completely melt before adding more.
5. Set it aside and allow the chocolate to cool to 84°F. Once the chocolate has reached this temperature, reheat it briefly by placing the bowl back over the simmering water for about 10 seconds, or until it's between 89° and 91°F. *Do not let the temperature of the chocolate exceed 91°F.*
6. Remove the bowl from the heat once you have reached the correct temperature. The chocolate should be smooth and glossy, with no streaks.

ASHLEY'S TIP

Rolling truffles is a messy job! Keep damp paper towels nearby so you can easily wipe off your hands as needed.

continues on p. 192

TO ASSEMBLE

1. Before you begin, make sure you have enough room in your refrigerator for two baking sheets, as the truffles must be chilled before coating.
2. Line two large baking sheets with parchment paper and set them aside.
3. Measure 2 teaspoons of the truffle filling and quickly roll it between your hands to form a ball. Transfer to the prepared baking sheet, and repeat with all filling. Refrigerate the rolled truffles for at least 1 hour before dipping in the chocolate. Remove the chilled truffles from the refrigerator.
4. Using a fork or candy dipper, dip each truffle into the chocolate, then lift it up over the bowl, allowing excess to drip back into the bowl before dunking it back in again, then lifting it out and allowing excess to drip into the bowl. Once the truffle has been double dunked, carefully transfer it back to the prepared baking sheet. (Note: To temper properly, chocolate needs to stay at its working temperature. For this recipe, that's between 89° and 91°F.) If the chocolate falls below that temperature while you're dipping, pause and briefly reheat it to the working temperature.
5. Sprinkle the top of each truffle with the peppermint candy.
6. Set them aside to allow the chocolate to set before serving, about 1 hour.
7. Store truffles in an airtight container, at room temperature, for up to 2 weeks.

Dark Chocolate & Sea Salt Caramels | YIELDS ABOUT 2 DOZEN CARAMELS

I have good news and bad news. The good news? These dark chocolate–covered sea salt caramels are absolutely delicious! The bad news? These dark chocolate–covered sea salt caramels are absolutely delicious. Soft, chewy, and soooo chocolatey, it's hard to stop at one. Nay, impossible! So I like to invite a few girlfriends over when I make these (forced sharing), and serve them with a bold red wine. Chocolate, wine, and friends . . . I can't think of a better combination!

DARK CHOCOLATE CARAMELS

Nonstick cooking spray

1 cup (312 ml) sweetened condensed milk

1 cup (198 g) granulated sugar

½ cup (106 g) packed light brown sugar

¾ cup (234 ml) light corn syrup

1 stick (113 g) unsalted butter, cut into ¼-inch cubes, room temperature

6 ounces (170 g) 70% dark chocolate, finely chopped

¼ cup (57 ml) water

½ teaspoon fine sea salt

1 tablespoon (14 ml) Kahlúa liqueur

2 teaspoons pure vanilla extract

1 teaspoon espresso powder

FOR THE CARAMELS

1. Line a 9 x 5-inch loaf pan with parchment paper, allowing paper to overlap on two of the pan sides. Grease the parchment and any exposed pan with nonstick cooking spray. Set the pan aside.
2. Fill a small cup with cold water and place a pastry brush in it. This will be used to brush down the sides of the pan to avoid crystallization. Set the cup aside.
3. In a heavy-bottomed 3-quart saucepan, combine the condensed milk, both sugars, corn syrup, butter, chocolate, the ¼ cup of water, and salt.
4. Place over medium heat and cook, stirring often with a rubber spatula and washing down the sides of the pan with the pastry brush as needed, until both sugars have completely dissolved and the butter and chocolate have completely melted.
5. Increase the heat to medium-high and cook, stirring constantly, until the mixture registers 250°F on a candy thermometer. Remove the pan from the heat and whisk in the Kahlúa, vanilla, and espresso powder.
6. Pour the mixture into the prepared pan and cool at room temperature for 2 hours.
7. To slice, place the pan in the refrigerator and chill for 60 to 75 minutes (but not much longer as it will become impossible to cut).
8. Using the parchment paper handles, lift the block of caramel out of the pan. Place the block upside down on a clean cutting board. Peel off the parchment paper, then turn the block of caramel right side up.
9. Lightly grease a large, sharp knife with nonstick cooking spray. Slice the caramel into 1-inch squares.
10. When you are ready to coat the caramels, make the tempered chocolate

ASHLEY'S TIP

If you're new to candy making, this recipe might take you a few tries to perfect. That's because a lot of technique is involved. So be sure to read the recipe start to finish, twice, and make sure you have all the equipment and ingredients on hand. You will not get the desired result if you skip steps or make ingredient substitutions.

continues on p. 195

TEMPERED CHOCOLATE

24 ounces (681 g) 70% dark chocolate, finely chopped

1 tablespoon flaky sea salt, plus more as needed

FOR THE TEMPERED CHOCOLATE

1. Fill a medium saucepan one-third full with water and bring to simmer over moderate heat. On top of the pan place a heatproof bowl that fits snugly without the bottom of the bowl touching the water. Reduce the heat to low and place two-thirds of the chocolate into the bowl. Place a candy thermometer into the chocolate and let it melt, stirring frequently with a rubber spatula. *Do not let the temperature of the chocolate exceed 120°F.*

2. Once the chocolate has fully melted, carefully remove the bowl from the heat, but keep the pot of simmering water on the burner. Wipe the bottom of the bowl to remove any condensation.

3. Stir in the remaining chocolate, a little bit at a time, allowing what you've added to completely melt before adding more.

4. Set it aside and allow the chocolate to cool to 84°F. Once the chocolate has reached this temperature, reheat it briefly by placing the bowl back over the simmering water for about 10 seconds, or until it's between 89° and 91°F. *Do not let the temperature exceed 91°F!*

5. Remove the bowl from the heat once you have reached the correct temperature. The chocolate should be smooth and glossy, with no streaks.

TO ASSEMBLE

1. Line a large baking sheet with parchment paper and set it aside.

2. Using a fork or candy dipper, dip each caramel into the chocolate, then lift it up over the bowl, allowing excess chocolate to drip back into the bowl before dunking it back in again, then lifting it out and allowing excess to drip into the bowl. (Note: To temper properly, chocolate needs to stay at its working temperature. For this recipe, that's between 89° and 91°F.) If the chocolate falls below that temperature while you're dipping your caramels, stop dipping and briefly reheat it to the working temperature.

3. Once the caramel has been double dunked, carefully transfer it back to the prepared baking sheet. Sprinkle the top of each caramel with the sea salt.

4. Set them aside and allow the chocolate to set before serving, about 1 hour.

5. Store caramels in an airtight container, at room temperature, for up to 2 weeks.

Candy

Chocolate-Covered Almond Toffee | YIELDS ONE 10 X 12-INCH TRAY

I can't think of a more classic Christmas treat than almond toffee. And because I'm a chocolate lover, my version includes a thick layer of semisweet chocolate on top. We always have a container of this in our fridge, which is delightful . . . and dangerous!

1 tablespoon (14 ml) vegetable oil, for greasing

2 cups (340 g) whole raw unsalted almonds

2 sticks (227 g) unsalted butter

1 cup (198 g) granulated sugar

¼ cup (53 g) packed light brown sugar

¼ cup (57 ml) dark rum

3 tablespoons (57 ml) light corn syrup

1 tablespoon (14 ml) water

½ teaspoon fine sea salt

¼ teaspoon baking soda

8 ounces (227 g) good-quality semisweet chocolate chips (such as Ghirardelli® or Guittard®)

½ teaspoon flaky sea salt

1. Position a rack in the center of the oven. Preheat the oven to 350°F.
2. Lightly brush the bottom of a large rimmed baking sheet with the oil. Lightly grease both sides of an offset spatula with the oil. Set both aside.
3. Place the almonds on a separate large rimmed baking sheet and bake for 8 minutes, tossing at the halfway point, or until almonds are lightly golden (avoid dark brown spots). Cool for 10 minutes. Roughly chop the almonds and set them aside.
4. In a deep medium saucepan, combine the butter, both sugars, rum, corn syrup, water, and fine sea salt.
5. Cook over medium heat, stirring occasionally, until the butter has completely melted. Increase the heat to medium-high and continue cooking, without stirring, until the mixture registers 300°F on a candy thermometer.
6. Remove the pan from the heat and immediately add the baking soda and 1 cup (170 g) of the chopped almonds, stirring with a rubber spatula until well combined.
7. Immediately pour the toffee onto the oiled rimmed baking sheet and, using the prepared offset spatula, spread it into a 10 x 12-inch rectangle.
8. While the toffee is still hot, sprinkle it with an even layer of the chocolate chips. Allow it to sit for 2 minutes. Then, using a small offset spatula, spread the chocolate over the toffee, covering it completely. Sprinkle the remaining almonds and flaky sea salt over the melted chocolate.
9. Refrigerate the toffee for 1 hour, or until the chocolate is completely set.
10. Holding the toffee with a piece of wax paper, break it into rough pieces.
11. Store in an airtight container, in the refrigerator, for up to 1 week.

Coconut-Pecan Truffles | YIELDS ABOUT 2 DOZEN TRUFFLES

You know those coconut eggs available around Easter time? These are like a homemade truffle version, but totally elevated in flavor and texture! A touch of cinnamon and toasted pecans give these a festive feel, without overwhelming the coconut flavor.

COCONUT-PECAN TRUFFLES

8 ounces (227 g) full-fat cream cheese, room temperature

¼ cup (57 g) coconut oil, soft enough to scoop

4 tablespoons (57 g) unsalted butter, room temperature

7¼ cups (819 g) confectioners' sugar, plus more if needed

1 cup (113 g) toasted pecans, finely chopped

½ teaspoon pure vanilla extract

½ teaspoon coconut extract

½ teaspoon salt

⅛ teaspoon ground cinnamon

11 ounces (312 g) sweetened shredded coconut

CHOCOLATE COATING

20 ounces (568 g) 70% dark chocolate, finely chopped

1 tablespoon (14 ml) coconut oil

48 small pecan halves or pieces, for garnish (optional)

1 tablespoon (14 g) flaky sea salt, for garnish (optional)

FOR THE TRUFFLES

1. Line a large baking sheet with parchment paper and set it aside.
2. In the bowl of a stand mixer fitted with the paddle attachment, or in a large bowl using a handheld electric mixer, combine the cream cheese, coconut oil, and butter. Beat on medium speed until well combined, scraping down the sides and bottom of the bowl as needed.
3. Reduce the mixer speed to low and gradually add the confectioners' sugar, about 1 cup (114 g) at a time. Once all the confectioners' sugar has been added, increase the speed to medium and add the pecans, vanilla, coconut extract, salt, and cinnamon, and continue beating until fully combined.
4. Add the shredded coconut and beat until evenly combined, scraping down the sides and bottom of the bowl as needed.
5. Place the mixture in the refrigerator to chill for exactly 1 hour. Remove the bowl from the fridge and scoop out heaping tablespoons (about 20 g) and roll into balls. Transfer to the prepared baking sheet.
6. Cover lightly with plastic wrap and place the pan in the freezer for 1 hour. About 15 minutes before you're ready to dip, make the chocolate coating.

FOR THE COATING

1. Fill a medium saucepan one-third full with water and bring to a simmer over moderate heat. On top of the pan place a heatproof bowl that fits snugly without the bottom of the bowl touching the water. Reduce the heat to the low.
2. Place the chocolate and coconut oil into the bowl and cook, stirring occasionally with a rubber spatula, until completely melted.
3. Carefully remove the bowl from the pan, ensuring no water comes in contact with the chocolate. Place one truffle onto a fork or candy dipper, and dip it into the melted chocolate, completely submerging it before pulling it back up. Allow excess chocolate to drip back into the bowl, then transfer it back to the parchment paper lined baking sheet. Gently press a piece of pecan on top of the wet chocolate, and sprinkle with flaky sea salt, if desired. Repeat with all truffles.
4. Set them aside until chocolate has completely set, about 2 hours.
5. Store truffles in an airtight container, in the refrigerator, for up to 5 days (see Tip).
6. When ready to serve, place each truffle in a truffle wrapper or arrange on a large serving platter (see Tip).

ASHLEY'S TIP

To store neatly, arrange the truffles in a large airtight container, placing them in a single layer, being sure to leave space between them. If you need to add a second layer, place a piece of wax paper on top of the first layer, then arrange in another single layer on top. You can avoid finger marks on the chocolate by using a piece of wax paper or plastic wrap, to move them.

Peppermint Bark | YIELDS ONE 9 X 13-INCH TRAY

Just look at those swirls! Aren't they hypnotizing? And this classic candy isn't just a looker. The combination of dark chocolate, white chocolate, and peppermint is absolutely delicious . . . and just screams "Christmas is coming"!

24 ounces (681 g) 70% dark chocolate, finely chopped

10 ounces (284 g) good-quality white chocolate, finely chopped

¾ teaspoon peppermint extract

¼ teaspoon salt

6 to 8 candy canes, crushed

1. Line a 9 x 13-inch pan with two layers of parchment paper, allowing paper to overlap on two of the sides.
2. Fill a medium saucepan one-third full with water and bring to a simmer over moderate heat. On top of the pan place a heatproof bowl that fits snugly without the bottom of the bowl touching the water. Reduce the heat to the low.
3. Place the dark chocolate into the bowl and cook, stirring frequently with a rubber spatula, until completely melted.
4. Carefully remove the bowl from the pan, making sure no water comes in contact with the chocolate.
5. Pour the melted dark chocolate into the prepared baking pan and spread into an even layer. Set pan aside.
6. On top of the pan, place another heatproof bowl that fits snugly without the bottom of the bowl touching the water.
7. Place the white chocolate, peppermint extract, and salt into the bowl and cook, stirring frequently with a rubber spatula, until completely melted.
8. Drizzle the white chocolate mixture on top of the melted dark chocolate, drizzling in long, parallel lines. Aim to get around 6 lines, and don't worry if they're a little messy and uneven.
9. Use a toothpick, skewer, or thin bladed knife to swirl the layers together. Go slow so you don't swirl too much and lose the design. Sprinkle the top of the bark with crushed candy canes.
10. Allow the chocolate to fully set at room temperature in a cool, dry place, about 4 hours.
11. Using a large, sharp knife, cut the bark into 3-inch pieces and serve at room temperature.
12. Store the bark in an airtight container, in the refrigerator, for up to 1 week.

ASHLEY'S TIP

Swirl slowly when combining the two chocolates. You can always swirl more, but over-swirling can create a messy look, which is why slow and steady creates the perfect balance.

8
CHAPTER

Cocktails & Beverages

In my family, we love hosting holiday happy hours. It's an easy excuse to gather friends together and enjoy a cup (or two) of holiday cheer! This chapter is dedicated to indulgent drinks, classic cocktails, and party punches perfect for your at-home celebrations. Every recipe has a fun twist, and includes gorgeous garnish ideas to make your festive drinks look just as good as they taste. Cheers!

European-Style Hot Chocolate with Peppermint Marshmallows | 204

Holiday Sangria | 208

Thick & Creamy Eggnog | 211

Pomegranate Party Punch | 212

Rosemary Lemonade | 215

Cranberry-Ginger Moscow Mules | 216

Cozy Mulled Cider | 219

Bloody Mary Brunch Bar | 220

Piña Colada Sunrise Mimosas | 223

European-Style Hot Chocolate with Peppermint Marshmallows | SERVES 8 TO 10

The best part about making homemade hot chocolate? You get to control exactly just how chocolatey your cocoa will be! As a die-hard chocolate fan, it's probably no surprise I opted for a ton of chocolate. This recipe calls for an entire pound (!) of chocolate and is similar to the thick drinking chocolate I've enjoyed in various cities around Europe. And because hot chocolate and marshmallows belong together, I've also included a homemade recipe for soft and chewy peppermint marshmallows.

HOT CHOCOLATE

4¼ cups (965 ml) whole milk

1½ cups (340 ml) heavy cream

2 tablespoons (14 g) confectioners' sugar

1 tablespoon (14 g) packed light brown sugar

1 tablespoon (14 g) unsalted butter

1 teaspoon espresso powder (optional)

¼ teaspoon fine sea salt

16 ounces (454 g) 70% dark chocolate, finely chopped

1½ tablespoons (21 ml) pure vanilla extract

PEPPERMINT MARSHMALLOWS
YIELDS ONE 9 X 9-INCH PAN

Nonstick cooking spray

¼ cup (28 g) confectioners' sugar, plus more for dusting

3 (0.25-g) packets unflavored powdered gelatin

¾ cup (170 ml) water, divided

1½ cups (298 g) granulated sugar

¾ cup (234 ml) light corn syrup

½ teaspoon salt

1 teaspoon peppermint extract

½ teaspoon pure vanilla extract

8 drops red food coloring, plus more if needed

Whipped Cream (page 211)

FOR THE HOT CHOCOLATE

1. In a medium saucepan, whisk together the milk, cream, both sugars, butter, espresso powder (if using), and salt. Place over medium heat and cook just until bubbles begin to form around the edges and the mixture begins to simmer; do not bring to a rolling boil.

2. Remove the saucepan from the heat and add the chocolate, whisking well until the chocolate is completely melted and incorporated.

3. Return the saucepan to low heat and cook, whisking constantly, for 5 more minutes, or until super thick and smooth. Stir in the vanilla, whisk well to combine, and cook for 1 more minute. Remove from heat.

4. Serve warm, topped with peppermint marshmallows and/or lots of freshly whipped cream! Hot chocolate will keep, stored covered in the refrigerator, for up to 48 hours. Reheat in the microwave or on the stovetop before drinking.

PEPPERMINT MARSHMALLOWS

1. Generously grease the bottom and sides of a 9 x 9-inch baking pan with nonstick cooking spray. Grease a rubber spatula with nonstick cooking spray. Coat the entire pan with a generous sprinkling of confectioners' sugar, then shake out any excess. Set it aside.

2. In the bowl of a stand mixer fitted with the whisk attachment, or in a large bowl using a handheld electric mixer, combine the gelatin and ½ cup (113 g) of the water. Beat on low speed until combined, then turn the mixer off and let the mixture sit until very firm, 10 to 12 minutes.

3. In a medium saucepan, combine the granulated sugar, corn syrup, salt, and the remaining ¼ cup (57 g) water. Bring to a simmer over medium heat and cook, stirring constantly, until the sugar is completely dissolved, about 5 minutes.

4. Increase the heat to medium-high and bring to a boil. Continue cooking for about 10 minutes, without stirring, until the mixture reaches 240°F on a candy thermometer. Remove the pan from the heat.

continues on p. 207

5. With the mixer on low speed, carefully pour the hot syrup, in a slow and steady stream, into the bowl containing the gelatin mixture. Once all the syrup has been added, increase the speed to high and beat about 10 minutes, until the mixture has tripled in volume and is very thick.

6. Add the peppermint extract and vanilla and beat for 2 more minutes.

7. Working very quickly, use the greased spatula to scrape the marshmallow mixture into the prepared baking dish and smooth the top.

8. Drop very small dots of the red food coloring evenly over the top and, using a toothpick or small skewer, lightly swirl to create a pretty marbled pattern.

9. Allow the mixture to sit, uncovered, at room temperature, for at least 5 hours, or up to 12 hours.

10. Dust a large cutting board generously with confectioners' sugar. Then loosen the sides of the marshmallows with a lightly greased knife. Invert them onto the cutting board, then dust the top of the marshmallows with more confectioners' sugar.

11. Using a generously greased chef's knife dusted with confectioners' sugar, cut the marshmallow slab into 1-inch pieces, dusting the knife with additional confectioners' sugar as needed (when it starts to catch on the marshmallows). Dust each marshmallow in additional confectioners' sugar, shaking off any excess sugar, before transferring them to a clean plate or container.

12. The marshmallows will keep, stored in an airtight container, at room temperature, for 1 month.

ASHLEY'S TIP

You can easily cut the hot chocolate recipe in half if you needed a smaller batch. Leftovers can be stored in the fridge, in an airtight container, for up to 48 hours. Reheat in the microwave or on the stovetop before drinking.

Cocktails & Beverages

Holiday Sangria | SERVES 4 TO 6

There's so much to love about this holiday sangria. But here are a few of the things I love most: It's beautiful, it serves a crowd, it's infinitely adaptable, and it tastes absolutely delicious! The secret ingredient: cinnamon simple syrup—so don't skip it! Don't like it too sweet? Start by adding half the syrup, tasting, and adding more to taste.

CINNAMON SIMPLE SYRUP

½ cup (99 g) granulated sugar
½ cup (113 ml) water
2 cinnamon sticks

SANGRIA

1 bottle (750 ml) dry red wine, such as Cabernet Sauvignon
1 cup (227 ml) pomegranate juice
1 cup (227 ml) unsweetened cranberry juice
½ cup (113 ml) Grand Marnier® liqueur
1 large Honeycrisp apple, cored and thinly sliced
1 large semi-firm Bartlett pear, cored and thinly sliced
2 small oranges, halved and thinly sliced
¾ cup (74 g) fresh cranberries
½ cup (70 g) pomegranate arils

GARNISHES

Cinnamon sticks
Sprigs of fresh rosemary
Pomegranate arils
Cranberries
Apple slices
Orange slices
Pear slices

FOR THE SIMPLE SYRUP

1. In a small saucepan, combine the sugar and water. Bring to a boil over medium-high heat. Cook, stirring frequently, until the sugar is completely dissolved, about 5 minutes. Add the cinnamon sticks and cook for another 5 minutes.

2. Remove the pan from the heat and set it aside to cool for 30 minutes, then remove the cinnamon sticks and transfer the simple syrup into an airtight container. Store in the refrigerator for at least 2 hours, and up to 2 weeks. Stir well before using.

FOR THE SANGRIA

1. In a large pitcher, combine the red wine, pomegranate juice, cranberry juice, Grand Marnier®, and all of the cinnamon simple syrup, stir well to combine.

2. Stir in the apple, pear, oranges, cranberries, and pomegranate arils. Cover and refrigerate for 4 to 6 hours before serving.

3. Serve chilled, garnished with fruit slices, cinnamon sticks, and/or rosemary sprigs.

Thick & Creamy Eggnog | SERVES 8 TO 10

Growing up, eggnog was a Christmas Eve tradition in our house. I always liked it, but my mom and brother loved it! And could easily consume multiple glasses in one night. I don't think I'll ever reach their level of eggnog enthusiasm. But I sure do love a small glass . . . especially with a big splash of bourbon and a swirl of whipped cream on top.

EGGNOG

10 large egg yolks

1½ cups (298 g) granulated sugar

8 cups (1.8 l) whole milk

1 cup (227 ml) heavy cream

2 tablespoons (28 ml) pure vanilla extract

1 teaspoon freshly grated nutmeg

1½ cups (340 ml) bourbon, rum, or brandy

WHIPPED CREAM

2 cups (454 ml) heavy cream

¼ cup (28 g) confectioners' sugar, sifted

GARNISH

Cinnamon sticks

Freshly grated nutmeg

FOR THE EGGNOG

1. In a large bowl, combine the egg yolks and sugar and whisk until well combined, about 1 minute. The mixture should be very thick and yellow. Set it aside.

2. In a large saucepan over medium-high heat, warm the milk just until bubbles begin to form around the edges; do not bring to a rolling boil.

3. Remove the pan from the heat and slowly pour 1 cup (227 ml) of the warm milk into the egg mixture, whisking constantly. Continue adding the milk to the egg mixture, 1 cup at a time and whisking constantly, until all the milk has been added. Then return this mixture back to the pan.

4. Return the pan to the stove and cook over medium-low heat, whisking constantly, until it's thick enough to coat the back of a spoon and registers 160°F on a thermometer.

5. Remove the pan from the heat and pour the mixture into a large heatproof bowl. Slowly whisk in the cream, stirring well to combine. Then whisk in the vanilla, nutmeg, and alcohol.

6. Cool the eggnog to room temperature, then pour it into a large pitcher and refrigerate for at least 6 hours before serving. Eggnog will keep, stored covered in the refrigerator, for up to 48 hours. Whisk well before serving.

FOR THE WHIPPED CREAM

1. Make the whipped cream right before serving! In the bowl of a stand mixer fitted with the whisk attachment, or in a large bowl using a handheld electric mixer, beat the cream and confectioners' sugar on medium-high speed until soft peaks form.

2. Right before serving, fold 1 cup of the whipped cream into the eggnog mixture, mixing just until combined.

3. Reserve the remaining whipped cream to dollop or pipe on top.

TO SERVE

1. Top each glass of eggnog with a dollop of whipped cream, a sprinkle of freshly grated nutmeg, and a cinnamon stick. Serve at once.

ASHLEY'S TIP

The secret to achieving the perfect eggnog texture? Cooking it to exactly 160°F, which is why I recommend using a digital or candy thermometer for this recipe.

Pomegranate Party Punch | SERVES 10 TO 12

Ready to party? Then bust out the punch bowl and whip up this sparkling pomegranate cocktail! Featuring festive flavors like pomegranate, pear, and ginger and spiked with tequila, Cointreau®, and Champagne, this drink is a total party starter. And the pretty star anise ice cubes are guaranteed to get plenty of "oohs and aahs" from your guests.

STAR ANISE ICE CUBES

12 star anise pods

Water

LEMON-LIME-GINGER SIMPLE SYRUP

1 cup (198 g) granulated sugar

1 cup (227 ml) water

8 ounces (230 g) fresh ginger, peeled and roughly chopped

¼ cup (57 ml) fresh lemon juice

¼ cup (57 ml) fresh lime juice

POMEGRANATE CHAMPAGNE PUNCH

3 cups (681 ml) pomegranate juice

1 cup (227 ml) pear nectar

1 cup (227 ml) tequila blanco

½ cup (113 ml) Cointreau® liqueur

2 (750-ml) bottles of Champagne or prosecco, chilled

GARNISH

¾ cup (105 g) pomegranate arils

3 sprigs fresh rosemary, trimmed

2 large oranges or blood oranges, thinly sliced

FOR THE ICE CUBES

1. In a 12-cavity (preferably extra-large) ice cube tray, place one star anise pod in each cavity. Cover the pods with water, filling the tray to the top.

2. Cover and place on a flat surface in the freezer. Freeze until completely solid.

FOR THE SYRUP

1. In a medium saucepan, combine the sugar, water, and ginger. Bring to a boil over medium-high heat and cook, stirring frequently, until the sugar is completely dissolved. Reduce the heat to medium-low and continue cooking, stirring occasionally, for 10 minutes.

2. Remove the pan from the heat, stir in the lemon juice and lime juice, and set it aside to cool for at least 1 hour.

3. Once the syrup is cool, strain it through a fine-mesh strainer and pour into an airtight container. Store in the refrigerator for at least 2 hours and up to 2 weeks.

FOR THE PUNCH

1. In a large punch bowl, combine the pomegranate juice, pear nectar, tequila, and Cointreau® and stir well to combine. Stir in all of the chilled simple syrup.

2. Right before serving, pour in the Champagne or prosecco and garnish with pomegranate arils, rosemary sprigs, and orange slices. Add star anise ice cubes as needed, or serve in a chilled bucket on the side.

ASHLEY'S TIP

Make sure all your liquid ingredients are prechilled before assembling the punch. Cold liquids will help keep the star anise ice cubes afloat longer, and keep the punch better chilled in the long run. Even with well-chilled liquids, you should assemble right before your guests arrive, and wait until the last minute to add the ice.

Rosemary Lemonade | SERVES 8

Let's start making lemonade a winter thing, okay? Specifically, this rosemary lemonade, which is utterly refreshing and full of fresh rosemary flavor. I like to make a big batch and put it on my bar cart, along with a few bottles of sparkling water, as a nonalcoholic drink option for my guests. That said, you can certainly spike it with some gin or vodka!

ROSEMARY SIMPLE SYRUP

2 cups (396 g) granulated sugar

2 cups (454 ml) water

9 sprigs fresh rosemary

2 (1-inch) strips lemon peel

LEMONADE

4 cups (908 ml) water

3 cups (681 ml) fresh lemon juice

1 cup (227 ml) Hendrick's® Gin (optional)

Lemon slices, for garnish

8 sprigs fresh rosemary, for garnish

FOR THE SYRUP

1. In a medium saucepan, combine the sugar, water, rosemary, and lemon peel. Bring to a simmer over medium heat and cook, stirring frequently, until the sugar is completely dissolved and the rosemary is fragrant, about 5 minutes.

2. Remove the pan from the heat and set it aside to cool for at least 1 hour.

3. When cool, strain through a fine-mesh strainer, discard the rosemary, and pour into an airtight container.

4. Store in the refrigerator for at least 1 hour and up to 2 weeks.

FOR THE LEMONADE

1. In a large pitcher, combine the simple syrup, water, and lemon juice. Stir well to combine and chill for at least 2 hours before serving.

2. When ready to serve, stir in the gin, if using. Then fill the glasses halfway with ice. Pour the lemonade over the ice and garnish each glass with a lemon slice and a rosemary sprig. Serve at once.

ASHLEY'S TIP

Unsure about the flavor of rosemary? Feel free to reduce the amount used in the simple syrup to 5 sprigs, which will yield a more subtle rosemary flavor. If you like it, you can always add more the next time!

Cranberry-Ginger Moscow Mules | SERVES 12

Moscow Mules are a Christmas tradition in our house. My husband and I make them every year, specifically on the night we decorate our tree. It's simple and special and something I look forward to all year long. This cranberry-ginger version is the perfect combination of tart and sweet, and can easily be made into a mocktail by omitting the alcohol. Just don't skip the garnish—fresh cranberries, mint sprigs, and lime wedges make these hot pink cocktails absolutely stunning!

GINGER-LIME SIMPLE SYRUP

2 cups (396 g) granulated sugar

2 cups (454 ml) water

2 (3-inch) strips lime peel

8 ounces (230 g) fresh ginger, peeled and roughly chopped

½ cup (113 ml) fresh lime juice

2 sprigs fresh mint

FOR EACH DRINK

2 tablespoons (28 ml) fresh lime juice

Ice

3 tablespoons (42 ml) vodka

3 tablespoons (42 ml) unsweetened cranberry juice

2 tablespoons (28 ml) Ginger-Lime Simple Syrup

1½ tablespoons (21 ml) Grand Marnier®

4 ounces (113 ml) ginger beer

GARNISHES

Lime wedges or spirals

Sprigs of fresh mint

Fresh cranberries

FOR THE SYRUP

1. In a medium saucepan, combine the sugar, water, lime peel, and ginger. Bring to a simmer over medium-high heat and cook, stirring frequently, until the sugar is completely dissolved. Then reduce the heat to medium-low and continue cooking, stirring occasionally, for 20 minutes.

2. Remove the pan from the heat, add the lime juice and mint, and set it aside to cool for at least 1 hour.

3. Once the syrup is cool, strain it through a fine-mesh strainer, and pour into an airtight container. Store in the refrigerator for at least 2 hours and up to 2 weeks.

TO ASSEMBLE

1. Pour the lime juice into a large glass or copper mule mug. Fill the glass ¾ full with ice.

2. Top with the vodka, cranberry juice, ginger-lime simple syrup, Grand Marnier®, and ginger beer. Gently stir, then top with a lime wedge or spiral, a sprig of mint, and a few cranberries. Repeat for as many guests as needed (you'll have enough simple syrup to make about a dozen cocktails). Serve at once.

ASHLEY'S TIP

Ginger beer varies brand to brand, in terms of both taste and carbonation. Since this ingredient plays a huge role in the flavor of this cocktail, I suggest taste-testing a few and finding your favorite!

Cozy Mulled Cider | SERVES 4 TO 6

A magical thing happens when you combine apple cider and spices in a saucepan and let them simmer away for a good amount of time: The mixture slowly builds flavor, and eventually transforms into the beloved cozy drink many of us know as mulled cider! My version includes all the familiar ingredients, plus maple syrup and citrus, which sweeten things up and add the perfect amount of brightness. Booze can be added but is totally optional.

CIDER

½ gallon (1.89 l) apple cider
¼ cup (57 ml) fresh lemon juice
¼ cup (57 ml) fresh orange juice
2 tablespoons (40 ml) pure maple syrup
12 whole green cardamom pods
6 cinnamon sticks
6 whole cloves
4 star anise pods
1 (3-inch) piece fresh ginger, peeled and sliced into ¼-inch chunks
⅛ teaspoon salt
1 cup (227 ml) rum, bourbon, or brandy (optional)

GARNISHES (OPTIONAL)

Cinnamon sticks
Star anise pods
Fresh rosemary
Orange slices
Lemon slices

1. In a large pot, combine the apple cider, lemon juice, orange juice, maple syrup, cardamom pods, cinnamon sticks, cloves, star anise, ginger, and salt. Bring to a boil over high heat, then immediately reduce the heat to medium-low and simmer, stirring occasionally, for 45 minutes. Stir in the alcohol, if using, and cook for 10 more minutes. Remove the pot from the heat.

2. Line a large fine-mesh strainer with a piece of cheesecloth, then place it over a very large heatproof bowl. Carefully strain the cider into the bowl. Discard the cheesecloth and whole spices.

3. Ladle the cider into mugs, garnish as desired, and serve warm.

ASHLEY'S TIP

Be sure to use apple cider, not apple cider vinegar!

Bloody Mary Brunch Bar | SERVES 6 TO 8

Looking to make your next brunch bash a real hit? Set up a Bloody Mary Bar! Don't worry—it's easier than it sounds. You can make the Bloody Mary mix up to 6 hours in advance and store it in the fridge, and most of the garnishes can be bought prepared or take just moments to whip up. Half the fun is letting guests assemble their own creations, so all you have to do is place everything out and let them play mixologist!

BLOODY MARY MIX

6 cups (1.4 l) tomato juice

¼ cup (57 ml) fresh lemon juice

¼ cup (57 ml) fresh lime juice

2½ tablespoons (50 g) prepared horseradish

2½ tablespoons (35 ml) Worcestershire sauce

1 tablespoon (14 g) tomato paste

1 tablespoon (14 g) finely grated yellow onion

2 teaspoons packed light brown sugar

1½ teaspoons Tabasco® sauce

1 teaspoon fine sea salt

1 teaspoon freshly ground black pepper

½ teaspoon garlic powder

2 cups (454 ml) vodka

OLD BAY® RIM

½ cup Old Bay® seasoning

8 lime wedges

GARNISH

Old Bay® seasoning

Celery

Pepperoncini

Crispy bacon slices

Gherkins

Boiled shrimp

Lemon wedges

Lime slices

Olives

Jalapeño peppers

Tabasco®

FOR THE MIX

1. In the body of a blender, combine the tomato juice, lemon juice, lime juice, horseradish, Worcestershire, tomato paste, onion, brown sugar, Tabasco®, salt, pepper, and garlic powder. Blend until smooth.

2. Pour into a large pitcher and refrigerate for up to 6 hours.

3. When you're ready to serve, remove the pitcher from the fridge, and stir in the vodka.

FOR THE RIM

1. Pour the Old Bay® seasoning into a wide, shallow dish.

2. Run a lime wedge around the edge of a glass, then dip it into the seasoning. Repeat with the remaining glasses.

3. Fill the glasses with ice, then top with the Bloody Mary mix. Allow your guests to garnish as desired (see below).

TO SERVE

1. Place garnishes in assorted bowls, cups, and dishes. Encourage your guests to dig in and create their perfect brunch Bloody Mary!

ASHLEY'S TIP

Consider serving the vodka on the side so guests have the option of making a Virgin Bloody Mary. Another reason to serve the booze on the side? You can set out a variety of flavored vodkas for your guests to sample.

Piña Colada Sunrise Mimosas | SERVES 6

Anyone can make a mimosa! It's literally just Champagne with a splash of orange juice. So here is a more elevated version perfect for Christmas morning, brunch, or any time you want a special celebration drink! The pineapple juice and coconut rum create the "piña colada" element, while a drizzle of grenadine creates a beautiful "sunrise" effect.

½ cup (99 g) coarse sugar

2 lime wedges

1 cup (227 ml) fresh orange juice

1 cup (227 ml) pineapple juice

¼ cup (57 ml) Malibu® rum

1 bottle (750 ml) Champagne or prosecco, chilled

¼ cup (57 ml) grenadine

¼ cup (35 g) pomegranate arils

8 sprigs fresh rosemary (optional)

1. Place the sugar in a small shallow bowl. Run a lime wedge around the rim of a Champagne flute, then dip it into the sugar. Repeat with the remaining flutes.

2. In a large glass measuring cup or pitcher, combine the orange juice, pineapple juice, and rum.

3. Divide the bottle of Champagne evenly among the six flutes, filling each about halfway full. Top each flute with the orange-pineapple juice mixture, filling until the flutes are a little more than three-quarters full. Slowly and carefully, spoon 2 teaspoons of grenadine into each flute. This should create a pretty layered color effect.

4. Garnish the with pomegranate arils and rosemary sprigs, if using, and serve at once!

ASHLEY'S TIP

The exact yield of this recipe will vary depending on the size of your glasses. If you're planning on serving more than four people or plan on serving more than one mimosa per person, I suggest having enough ingredients on hand to make two rounds!

Cocktails & Beverages

PART THREE

Entertaining 101

Baking Secrets

The world of baking is a magical place . . . especially during the holidays! But before you dive into any of my baking recipes, I want to share some secrets—and important information—that will set you up for success.

1. **Read the entire recipe—including the ingredient list—before you begin baking!** If it's a more complicated recipe, or one with techniques you've never tried before, I recommend reading it twice. This will not only make you feel more confident once you start baking, but will ensure you have all the tools and time required to complete the recipe from start to finish.
2. **Follow the recipe *exactly* as it's written!** This means no skipping steps or substituting ingredients, unless specified in the recipe. It can be fun to experiment, but when you do this in baking, you risk ruining the entire recipe. Baking is a science, so precision is everything!
3. **Use a digital kitchen scale!** This tool will instantly improve your baking and give you more consistent results. It's also the only way I can guarantee your recipes will come out looking and tasting exactly like the ones you see in these photos. Follow the weight measurements listed and you'll be golden!
4. **If you're not going to use a digital scale, measure your flour correctly!** First, fluff up the flour. Use a spoon to loosen up the flour while it's in the bag or container. Next, very lightly spoon the flour into the measuring cup. Continue spooning the flour into the cup until it's over filling the cup, then use the flat edge of a knife to scrape the excess flour off the cup, back into the container. Measure the flour this way for each cup of flour called for.

5. **Have the proper equipment on hand!** Most of the tools called for in this book are items you likely already have in your kitchen: baking sheets, measuring cups and spoons, mixing bowls, and utensils like spatulas, whisks, and cookie scoops. But certain recipes call for more specific tools, like a food processor or a candy thermometer. These tools are essential to those recipes, so be sure to obtain them before you begin baking.

6. **Invest in an oven thermometer!** They're very affordable and, much like a digital kitchen scale, can instantly improve your baking. Home ovens are notoriously off temperature: your oven may tell you it's 350°F, but isn't actually! Most ovens vary by 15 to 20 degrees, but in baking, even that small amount can make a big difference.

7. **Pay attention to temperature!** If a recipe calls for cold butter, make sure it's *really* cold. If you live in a warm climate, you may need to place the butter in the freezer for ten to fifteen minutes before you begin baking to ensure it doesn't soften too quickly as you assemble your recipe. Alternatively, if a recipe calls for eggs at room temperature, ensure you take the eggs out of the fridge at least 30 minutes before you start baking. This attention to detail will make a huge difference in how your ingredients bond, which in turn makes a huge impact of the overall success of the recipe.

8. **Make sure the ingredients are fresh!** From flour, to leavening agents (baking powder, baking soda, and yeast), to spices and nuts, fresh ingredients make all the difference. Some stale or expired ingredients may only affect the taste—for instance, if you use old spices like cinnamon or nutmeg in cookies. This won't ruin the recipe per se, but will yield less flavorful cookies than intended. However, expired baking soda, baking powder, or yeast can lead to recipe disaster. So a general rule of thumb is fresh is best!

9. **Baking times are only suggestions!** So, in addition to a time frame, most baking recipes include doneness indicators. For example, "Bake for 30 minutes, or until the brownies are set at the edges, shiny on top, and slightly jiggly in the center." The indicators are there because baking times can vary depending on several factors, including oven temperature, equipment, and even the weather! Did you know brownies can take 10 to 15 minutes longer to bake if you use a ceramic pan rather than a steel pan? So be sure to use your sensory indicators, along with your best judgment, to know when your recipe is ready to come out.

10. **Practice makes perfect!** Every time you roll out pie crust, bake a batch of cookies, or whip up a pan of brownies, you're becoming a better baker. You'll learn new tricks and techniques with each recipe, and eventually they'll become second nature. So, remember, even if it's not your best work, spending time in the kitchen is never a waste of time with the right perspective!

Ashley's Entertaining Tips

There's so much magic and joy to be found during the holiday season. But the excitement can also be accompanied by not-so-happy emotions like stress, anxiety, and overwhelm. Especially so, if you're new to the world of holiday entertaining. The good news? I'm here to help! Below are my top entertaining tips to help you craft a plan, stay focused, and create holiday happiness all season long. Keep in mind that not every tip will suit every person. So feel free to pick and choose the ones that will serve you best. More than anything, just remember to have fun!

1. **Make a plan and stick to it.**

    Planning is the first step—and most important part—of hosting any event. Whether you're hosting a last-minute cocktail party or a sit-down dinner for ten, you need a plan. Planning in advance will not only lower your stress level, but give you plenty of time to craft a great guest list and menu, send out your invites, and create a welcoming atmosphere for your guests. I suggest writing your plan down and sticking to it! It can be tempting to add "one more appetizer" to the menu or invite a few more guests, but sticking to your plan will save you time, money, and grief in the long run!

2. **Don't forget to plan time for you!**

   When you're crafting your "day of" timeline, don't forget to factor getting yourself ready into the day. Carve out at least 30 minutes when you can shower, do your hair, change your outfit, and/or anything else you'd like to do to feel refreshed, confident, and ready to receive your guests. I'll often do my hair in the morning because it's time-consuming, and lay out an outfit I can quickly change into right before my guests arrive (I don't know about you, but I don't want to socialize in the same outfit I cooked and cleaned in all day). That way, I'm 99 percent ready to go before I even start the day! Even if you're just planning on wearing casual attire or pajamas, it's nice to take a moment to yourself before your guests arrive.

3. **Choose a menu.**

   Menu planning can be so much fun! But if you're new to entertaining, planning a balanced spread can feel overwhelming. Don't fret! Simply reference my Holiday Party Menus (pages 6–11), and pick and choose the recipes that work best for you! Once you've selected your menu, write down all the ingredients you'll need and make sure you'll be able to easily find them. If there's anything that must be ordered in advance, make sure it will arrive well ahead of your party. If time and finances allow, I also suggest doing a trial run with your menu. This way you'll know exactly how much time it takes you to prepare the menu and how the dishes will come out.

4. **Decide on a theme.**

   Or, at the very least, decide what kind of event you're hosting. Will it be a simple brunch, a fancy sit-down dinner, or a casual cocktail party with a few neighbors and friends? Knowing this will make selecting your menu, choosing a date, setting a time, and creating the perfect ambience so much easier!

5. **Let your guests know if there's a dress code.**

   If you're having a casual "anything goes" event, mentioning a dress code might not be necessary. But if you plan on dressing up (or down), it's best to let your guests know so they can plan ahead and feel comfortable when they arrive. Whether you're hosting in Christmas pajamas, an ugly sweater, or a sparkly cocktail dress, relay that in your invite and give your guests an opportunity to join in on the fun! And if you're a "no shoes" household, definitely let your guests know in advance so they can wear socks they feel comfortable in.

6. **Include nonalcoholic drink options.**

   'Tis the season for cocktails—but in an effort to make all of your guests feel comfortable, set out *at least* one booze-free option with the wine and cocktails. Sparkling water (in a variety of flavors), iced tea (ginger and hibiscus are always hits), and homemade Rosemary Lemonade (page 215) are all great options! A few carafes of good old H_2O should also be easily accessible so all your guests can hydrate in between drinks.

7. **Don't forget to garnish!**

   A simple way to dress up your dishes is to add garnish. Whether you're making a handcrafted cocktail, a family-style platter, or a simple sheet cake, garnishes visually take dishes from looking good to looking *great*! These can be as simple as adding a sprig of rosemary, a few slices of lemon, or a sprinkling of fresh chives. Just make sure the garnish complements the flavors and theme of the dish. Use the photos and notes in this book as a guide on how to gorgeously garnish your recipes. And don't forget to add garnishes to your shopping list!

8. **Curate the perfect party playlist.**

   Music can make any party better! And the holidays are double the fun because you can create a playlist that combines party classics with holiday hits. I always suggest making the playlist 75 percent hits, and then adding in a handful of lesser-known tunes to play in between. (But this is my personal preference, so feel free to do it your way!) Just remember to keep the enjoyment of all guests in mind and create a playlist that will outlast your party. Also: keep the volume in check. While music can certainly enhance the atmosphere of your event, if it's too loud, it can also negatively impact the vibe.

Crafting a Guest List

Make a list . . . and check it twice! Every good party starts with a good guest list. While you may be tempted to invite every soul you know (which is very sweet and considerate), I suggest being very intentional about who you invite. A few questions to ask yourself as you create your list:

- **How many people can I comfortably host?** You should of course consider your space first, and decide how many people you can physically fit with ease. Do you have enough chairs if everyone wants to sit? What about table space? If you're hosting a casual cocktail party, having most of your guests stand is probably fine. But if you're serving a prime rib dinner, you'll need adequate space for each guest to sit and enjoy their meal. You should also consider the time you're willing to spend (preparing for a party can take hours, if not days), as well as the costs of providing food and drinks. A party of eight may not sound like a lot, but when you add up appetizers, cocktails, dinner, and dessert, it may exceed your intended budget. Better to do these calculations first so you can fully enjoy the planning and actual event.
- **Is there a good mix of personalities?** Everyone has their favorite friends or family members and that's a great starting point! Add those "must-invite" folks to your list first, then start considering the other potential guests. Once you have a good list, play a little game of imagination! Try to envision them all sitting in your living room or standing around your kitchen island. How are they getting along? Will conversation naturally ebb and flow? Is there a good mix of introverts and extroverts to keep things balanced? Having the right mix of personalities will not only create a delightful atmosphere for everyone at

your party, but takes the pressure off you as a host to individually entertain and check in on every guest.

- **Do I want children at this event?** If you don't, you should make this clear in your invitation—even if it's a nighttime event. And if any of your guests have grown children, you may also want to specify whether they're invited or not.

- **Are you prepared to accommodate multiple plus-ones?** If you're inviting someone who is married, or in a serious relationship, you should always invite their other half and consider them a "package deal." But what about single friends—is it safe to assume they'll come alone? In my opinion, you should never assume. Unless you're ready to accommodate multiple "surprise guests," you should clarify if you're comfortable with plus-ones.

- **Will anyone on this list add to my workload or prevent me from fully enjoying my party?** Being a great friend and being a great host are two very different things. If you have a friend or family member you know is going to be a handful, carefully consider whether inviting them is the right move. If you think the event will lift their spirits, brighten their mood, and be just the thing they need to awaken their holiday cheer, by all means, invite away! But if you think they may complain, offend other guests, get too drunk, or cause you grief and anxiety, consider leaving them off the list and planning a special day to spend with just that person. Not every event is meant for every person, and that's okay!

- **Does anyone have severe allergies or food restrictions I'll have to plan for?** This is a very important question! If one, or multiple, guests have allergies or don't eat certain foods, you may need to plan multiple menus and prep the food very strategically to ensure there's no cross-contamination. If you're okay with this, great! But if the idea of making multiple menus makes your skin itch with stress, it's something to consider before sending out your invitations.

The questions mentioned above aren't meant to persuade you to exclude anyone from your guest list; rather, they are simply things to consider as you plan your event. Surprises are not something you want popping up at the last minute. So be sure to be very clear with your invitations and try not to make too much work for yourself.

Acknowledgments

To my mom, the heartbeat of this book. It feels a little silly writing this since you won't get to read it, but there's no way I could begin this section without thanking you first. For your love, sacrifice, and dedication, I will always be grateful. Thank you for making every holiday feel like magic and for encouraging me to reach for my dreams. I carry you with me always.

To Charlie, the love of my life. Having you as a husband is truly the greatest gift and being with you makes every day feel like a holiday. Thank you for being my home . . . and for unloading the dishwasher and making the coffee every morning! I love you the most!

To Remi, I can't wait to become your mama! I love you so much already.

To Tessa Arias, my best friend, fellow baker, and holiday enthusiast. I love you and I'm so grateful for our sisterhood! What would life be like without you? I don't even want to imagine! I can't wait to create a million more memories together!

To LeAnna Weller Smith, aka the visionary who designed this gorgeous book! I'm so grateful Tessa introduced us and you're now a part of my world! Thank you for guiding me through this crazy process, making Zoom meetings fun, and listening to me complain about pregnancy insomnia with grace and compassion!

To Joanie Simon and Brendan McCaskey, my photography dream team! The photos you created and captured for this book not only brought my vision to life, but—as you both already know—made me cry tears of joy on several occasions. Thank you for always going the extra mile to make each shot pure perfection!

To my Rhinebeck crew, you're the best community of neighbors and friends a girl could ask for! Thank you for being my favorite taste-testers and party guests! Your kindness, acceptance, and encouragement are what makes our little village truly feel like home! I love you all!

To my friends and followers of Baker by Nature . . . *You are the reason this book exists!* I would not be where I am today without your loyalty, support, and love! Getting to share recipes with you is my greatest pleasure. I'm forever grateful to you!

Index

A

allergies & food restrictions, 234
allspice
   Gingerbread Celebration Cake, 149–150
   Molasses Cream Pies, 171–172
almonds
   Cherry-Almond Chocolate Bark, 182
   Chocolate-Covered Almond Toffee, 197
   Whipped Ricotta Toast with Olives & Almonds, 42
anchovy paste: Crowd-Pleasing Caesar Salad with Garlic Bread Croutons, 111–112
appetizers & snacks
   Brie Bites with Cranberry Chutney, 60–63
   Caramelized Onion Dip Snack Board, 51–52
   Four-Cheese Spinach Dip, 66
   Garlic Parmesan Popcorn, 55
   Italian Hoagie Party Platter, 59
   Lemon-Rosemary Chicken Wings, 45–46
   Mini Crab Cakes with Spicy Remoulade, 65
   Prosciutto-Wrapped Jalapeño Poppers, 56
   Ultimate Meatball Sliders, 47–48
   Whipped Ricotta Toast with Olives & Almonds, 42
apples
   Brie Bites with Cranberry Chutney, 60–63
   Cinnamon Apple French Toast, 35
   Cozy Mulled Cider, 219
   Holiday Sangria, 208
   Morning Glory Muffins, 39
   Salted Caramel Apple Pie Bars, 173–174
arugula
   Chicken Parmesan for a Crowd, 84–86
   Feel-Good Holiday Salad, 103
Asiago
   Garlicky Shrimp Polenta, 73
   Prosciutto-Wrapped Jalapeño Poppers, 56
   Ultimate Meatball Sliders, 47–48
avocados: Feel-Good Holiday Salad, 103

B

bacon
   Bacon & Caramelized Onion Quiche, 23–24
   Feel-Good Holiday Salad, 103
   Warm Bacon & Green Bean Salad, 115
Baked Ziti, Meatball & Spinach, 77–78
baking secrets, 227–229
Balsamic Roasted Brussels Sprouts with Pancetta & Pomegranate Seeds, 108
Banana-Double Chocolate Bundt Cake, 36
Bark, Cherry-Almond Chocolate, 182
Bark, Peppermint, 201
bars. *see* cookies & bars
basil
   Chicken Parmesan for a Crowd, 84–86
   Meatball & Spinach Baked Ziti, 77–78
   Rigatoni Bolognese with Garlic Bread, 87–89
   Ultimate Meatball Sliders, 47–48
beans
   Pasta Fagioli, 104
   Warm Bacon & Green Bean Salad, 115
beef
   Italian Wedding Soup, 97
   Special Occasion Roast Beef with Roasted Carrots, 83
   Ultimate Meatball Sliders, 47–48
Beignets, Nutella®, 25–27
bell peppers
   Garlicky Shrimp Polenta, 73
   Sausage & Potato Breakfast Casserole, 28
beverages. *see* cocktails & beverages
Biscotti, Cranberry-Pistachio, 163–164
Black Forest Cheesecake, 137–138
Blondies, Brown Butter, 179
Bloody Mary Brunch Bar, 220
blue cheese: Feel-Good Holiday Salad, 103
Bolognese, Rigatoni, with Garlic Bread, 87–89
bourbon
   Bourbon Butter Pecan Fudge, 185
   Bourbon Maple Syrup, 16

Brown Butter-Orange Ricotta
   Pancakes, 16
Cozy Mulled Cider, 219
Thick & Creamy Eggnog, 211
brandy
   Cozy Mulled Cider, 219
   Thick & Creamy Eggnog, 211
breakfast & brunch
   Bacon & Caramelized Onion Quiche, 23–24
   Bloody Mary Brunch Bar, 220
   Brown Butter-Orange Ricotta Pancakes, 16
   Cinnamon Apple French Toast, 35
   Cranberry Orange Scones, 32
   Cranberry-Pistachio Biscotti, 163–164
   Double Chocolate-Banana Bundt Cake, 36
   Fluffy Cinnamon Rolls, 19–20
   Morning Glory Muffins, 39
   Nutella® Beignets, 25–27
   Sausage & Potato Breakfast Casserole, 28
   Sugar & Spice Donuts, 31
Brie Bites with Cranberry Chutney, 60–63
Brown Butter Blondies, 179
Brown Butter-Orange Ricotta Pancakes, 16
Brownies, Triple Chocolate, 159
brunch. see breakfast & brunch
Brussels Sprouts, Balsamic Roasted, with Pancetta & Pomegranate Seeds, 108
Buns, Italian Asiago, 48
butter
   My Favorite Butter Cookies, 154–157
   Parker House Rolls, 98–101
buttermilk: Brown Butter-Orange Ricotta Pancakes, 16
Butter Pecan Fudge, Bourbon, 185

C

Caesar Salad with Garlic Bread Croutons, Crowd-Pleasing, 111–112
cakes
   Black Forest Cheesecake, 137–138
   Chocolate Peppermint Cake, 126–128
   Christmas Funfetti Sheet Cake, 133–134
   Double Chocolate-Banana Bundt Cake, 36
   Gingerbread Celebration Cake, 149–150
   New York-Style Cheesecake with Grand Marnier® Cranberry Sauce, 121–122
   Pumpkin Cheesecake with Pecan Praline Sauce, 129–130
   Sparkling Champagne Cupcakes, 141–142
candy
   Bourbon Butter Pecan Fudge, 185
   Cherry-Almond Chocolate Bark, 182
   Chocolate-Covered Almond Toffee, 197
   Chocolate-Covered Peanut Butter Christmas Trees, 186–189
   Coconut-Pecan Truffles, 198
   Dark Chocolate & Sea Salt Caramels, 193–195
   Kahlúa Peppermint Mocha Chocolate Truffles, 190–192
   see also cookies & Bars; desserts
candy canes
   Chocolate Peppermint Cake, 126–128
   Peppermint Bark, 201
Cannoli, Extra Creamy, 125
Caper-Lemon Sauce, Pan-Seared Cod in, 74
capicola: Italian Hoagie Party Platter, 59
Caramel Apple Pie Bars, Salted, 173–174
Caramelized Onion Dip Snack Board, 51–52
Caramels, Dark Chocolate & Sea Salt, 193–195
cardamom: Cozy Mulled Cider, 219
carrots
   Italian Wedding Soup, 97
   Morning Glory Muffins, 39
   Pasta Fagioli, 104
   Special Occasion Roast Beef with Roasted Carrots, 83
Casserole, Sausage & Potato Breakfast, 28

Champagne
   Piña Colada Sunrise Mimosas, 223
   Pomegranate Party Punch, 212
   Sparkling Champagne Cupcakes, 141–142
cheddar
   Creamy White Cheddar Macaroni & Cheese, 107
   Four-Cheese Spinach Dip, 66
   Prosciutto-Wrapped Jalapeño Poppers, 56
   Sausage & Potato Breakfast Casserole, 28
cheese
   Bacon & Caramelized Onion Quiche, 23–24
   Brie Bites with Cranberry Chutney, 60–63
   Chicken Parmesan for a Crowd, 84–86
   Creamy White Cheddar Macaroni & Cheese, 107
   Crowd-Pleasing Caesar Salad with Garlic Bread Croutons, 111–112
   Extra Creamy Cannoli, 125
   Feel-Good Holiday Salad, 103
   Four-Cheese Spinach Dip, 66
   Garlicky Shrimp Polenta, 73
   Garlic Parmesan Popcorn, 55
   Italian Hoagie Party Platter, 59
   Italian Wedding Soup, 97
   Lemon Risotto with Brown Butter Scallops, 79–80
   Meatball & Spinach Baked Ziti, 77–78
   Prosciutto-Wrapped Jalapeño Poppers, 56
   Ultimate Meatball Sliders, 47–48
   Whipped Ricotta Toast with Olives & Almonds, 42
   see also cream cheese; mascarpone
cheesecakes
   Black Forest Cheesecake, 137–138
   New York-Style Cheesecake with Grand Marnier® Cranberry Sauce, 121–122
   Pumpkin Cheesecake with Pecan Praline Sauce, 129–130
cherries
   Black Forest Cheesecake, 137–138

Index | 241

cherries (continued)
    Cherry-Almond Chocolate Bark, 182
    Cranberry Cherry Pie, 145–147
chicken
    Chicken Parmesan for a Crowd, 84–86
    Lemon-Rosemary Chicken Wings, 45–46
    see also Cornish game hens
chocolate
    Black Forest Cheesecake, 137–138
    Brown Butter Blondies, 179
    Cherry-Almond Chocolate Bark, 182
    Chocolate-Covered Almond Toffee, 197
    Chocolate-Covered Peanut Butter Christmas Trees, 186–189
    Chocolate Crinkles, 168
    Chocolate Ganache, 128
    Chocolate Glaze, 36
    Chocolate Peppermint Cake, 126–128
    Coconut-Pecan Truffles, 198
    Cranberry-Pistachio Biscotti, 163–164
    Dark Chocolate & Sea Salt Caramels, 193–195
    Double Chocolate-Banana Bundt Cake, 36
    Eggnog Tiramisu, 118
    European-Style Hot Chocolate with Peppermint Marshmallows, 204–207
    Extra Creamy Cannoli, 125
    Kahlúa Peppermint Mocha Chocolate Truffles, 190–192
    My Favorite Butter Cookies, 154–157
    Nutella® Beignets, 25–27
    Oatmeal Chocolate Chunk Cookies, 160
    Peanut Butter M&M® Cookies, 176
    Peppermint Bark, 201
    Triple Chocolate Brownies, 159
    see also candy; white chocolate
Christmas Funfetti Sheet Cake, 133–134
Christmas Trees, Chocolate-Covered Peanut Butter, 186–189
Chutney, Cranberry, 63
Cider, Cozy Mulled, 219
cinnamon
    Cinnamon Apple French Toast, 35
    Cinnamon Apple Syrup, 35
    Cinnamon Simple Syrup, 208
    Cozy Mulled Cider, 219
    Fluffy Cinnamon Rolls, 19–20
    Gingerbread Celebration Cake, 149–150
    Holiday Sangria, 208
    Molasses Cream Pies, 171–172
    Morning Glory Muffins, 39
    Nutella® Beignets, 25–27
    Salted Caramel Apple Pie Bars, 173–174
    Sugar & Spice Donuts, 31
cloves
    Cozy Mulled Cider, 219
    Molasses Cream Pies, 171–172
cocktails & beverages
    Bloody Mary Brunch Bar, 220
    Cozy Mulled Cider, 219
    Cranberry-Ginger Moscow Mules, 216
    European-Style Hot Chocolate with Peppermint Marshmallows, 204–207
    Holiday Sangria, 208
    nonalcoholic options, including, 232
    Pomegranate Party Punch, 212
    Rosemary Lemonade, 215
    Thick & Creamy Eggnog, 211
coconut: Morning Glory Muffins, 39
Cod, Pan-Seared, in Lemon-Caper Sauce, 74
coffee
    Eggnog Tiramisu, 118
    see also espresso powder; Kahlúa
Cointreau®: Pomegranate Party Punch, 212
condensed milk, sweetened
    Bourbon Butter Pecan Fudge, 185
    Dark Chocolate & Sea Salt Caramels, 193–195
condiments. see sauces & condiments
cookies & bars
    Brown Butter Blondies, 179
    Chocolate Crinkles, 168
    Cranberry-Pistachio Biscotti, 163–164
    Lemon White Chocolate Macadamia Nut Cookies, 167
    Molasses Cream Pies, 171–172
    My Favorite Butter Cookies, 154–157
    Oatmeal Chocolate Chunk Cookies, 160
    Peanut Butter M&M® Cookies, 176
    Salted Caramel Apple Pie Bars, 173–174
    Triple Chocolate Brownies, 159
    see also candy; desserts
Cornish game hens:
    Holiday Hens with Wild Rice Pilaf, 70
    see also chicken
Cozy Mulled Cider, 219
Crab Cakes, Mini, with Spicy Remoulade, 65
cranberries
    Brie Bites with Cranberry Chutney, 60–63
    Cranberry Cherry Pie, 145–147
    Cranberry-Ginger Moscow Mules, 216
    Cranberry Orange Scones, 32
    Cranberry-Pistachio Biscotti, 163–164
    Feel-Good Holiday Salad, 103
    Gingerbread Celebration Cake, 149–150
    Holiday Hens with Wild Rice Pilaf, 70
    Holiday Sangria, 208
    Morning Glory Muffins, 39
    New York-Style Cheesecake with Grand Marnier® Cranberry Sauce, 121–122
cream cheese
    Black Forest Cheesecake, 137–138
    Caramelized Onion Dip Snack Board, 51–52
    Christmas Funfetti Sheet Cake, 133–134
    Coconut-Pecan Truffles, 198
    Cream Cheese Frosting, 134, 172
    Cream Cheese Glaze, 19
    Extra Creamy Cannoli, 125
    Fluffy Cinnamon Rolls, 19–20
    Four-Cheese Spinach Dip, 66
    Molasses Cream Pies, 171–172
    New York-Style Cheesecake with Grand Marnier® Cranberry Sauce, 121–122
    Prosciutto-Wrapped Jalapeño Poppers, 56
    Pumpkin Cheesecake with Pecan Praline Sauce, 129–130

Sparkling Champagne Cupcakes, 141–142
see also mascarpone
Creamy White Cheddar Macaroni & Cheese, 107
Crinkles, Chocolate, 168
crostini
    Brie Bites with Cranberry Chutney, 60–63
    Four-Cheese Spinach Dip, 66
Cupcakes, Sparkling Champagne, 141–142

D
Dark Chocolate & Sea Salt Caramels, 193–195
desserts
    Black Forest Cheesecake, 137–138
    Chocolate Peppermint Cake, 126–128
    Christmas Funfetti Sheet Cake, 133–134
    Cranberry Cherry Pie, 145–147
    Double Chocolate-Banana Bundt Cake, 36
    Eggnog Tiramisu, 118
    Extra Creamy Cannoli, 125
    Gingerbread Celebration Cake, 149–150
    New York-Style Cheesecake with Grand Marnier® Cranberry Sauce, 121–122
    Nutella® Beignets, 25–27
    Pumpkin Cheesecake with Pecan Praline Sauce, 129–130
    Sparkling Champagne Cupcakes, 141–142
    Sugar & Spice Donuts, 31
    see also candy; cookies & bars
Dijon mustard: Special Occasion Roast Beef with Roasted Carrots, 83
dinners. *see* meals
Dip, Caramelized Onion, Snack Board, 51–52
Dip, Four-Cheese Spinach, 66
donuts
    Nutella® Beignets, 25–27
    Sugar & Spice Donuts, 31
    Double Chocolate-Banana Bundt Cake, 36
dress codes, 230
Dressing, Caesar, 111

E
Eggnog, Thick & Creamy, 211
Eggnog Tiramisu, 118
eggs
    Bacon & Caramelized Onion Quiche, 23–24
    Eggnog Tiramisu, 118
    New York-Style Cheesecake with Grand Marnier® Cranberry Sauce, 121–122
    Sausage & Potato Breakfast Casserole, 28
    Thick & Creamy Eggnog, 211
entertaining tips, 229–232
equipment, 228
espresso powder
    Black Forest Cheesecake, 137–138
    Chocolate Crinkles, 168
    Chocolate Peppermint Cake, 126–128
    Dark Chocolate & Sea Salt Caramels, 193–195
    Double Chocolate-Banana Bundt Cake, 36
    Gingerbread Celebration Cake, 149–150
    Kahlúa Peppermint Mocha Chocolate Truffles, 190–192
    Triple Chocolate Brownies, 159
European-Style Hot Chocolate with Peppermint Marshmallows, 204–207
evaporated milk: Nutella® Beignets, 25–27
Extra Creamy Cannoli, 125

F
fish. *see* seafood
Fluffy Cinnamon Rolls, 19–20
fontina
    Chicken Parmesan for a Crowd, 84–86
    Meatball & Spinach Baked Ziti, 77–78
    Prosciutto-Wrapped Jalapeño Poppers, 56
food restrictions & allergies, 234
Four-Cheese Spinach Dip, 66
French Toast, Cinnamon Apple, 35
frostings & icings
    Champagne Frosting, 142
    Chocolate Ganache, 128
    Cream Cheese Frosting, 134, 172
    Cream Cheese Glaze, 19
    Mascarpone Frosting, 150
    Orange Glaze, 32
    White Chocolate Peppermint Frosting, 126
Fudge, Bourbon Butter Pecan, 185

G
garlic
    Crowd-Pleasing Caesar Salad with Garlic Bread Croutons, 111–112
    Garlicky Shrimp Polenta, 73
    Garlic Parmesan Popcorn, 55
    Rigatoni Bolognese with Garlic Bread, 87–89
    Rosemary & Garlic Roasted Potatoes, 94
garnishes, 232
gin: Rosemary Lemonade, 215
ginger
    Cozy Mulled Cider, 219
    Cranberry-Ginger Moscow Mules, 216
    Gingerbread Celebration Cake, 149–150
    Molasses Cream Pies, 171–172
    Pomegranate Party Punch, 212
ginger beer: Brie Bites with Cranberry Chutney, 60–63
Gingerbread Celebration Cake, 149–150
glazes. *see* frostings & icings
graham cracker crumbs
    New York-Style Cheesecake with Grand Marnier® Cranberry Sauce, 121–122
    Pumpkin Cheesecake with Pecan Praline Sauce, 129–130
Grand Marnier®
    Cranberry-Ginger Moscow Mules, 216
    Holiday Sangria, 208
    New York-Style Cheesecake with Grand Marnier® Cranberry Sauce, 121–122
Green Bean & Bacon Salad, Warm, 115

grenadine: Piña Colada Sunrise
    Mimosas, 223
Gruyère
    Bacon & Caramelized Onion Quiche,
        23–24
    Creamy White Cheddar Macaroni &
        Cheese, 107
guest lists, 233–234

H

hazelnuts: Nutella® Beignets, 25–27
hens, Cornish game: Holiday Hens with
    Wild Rice Pilaf, 70
Herb-Crusted Salmon with Mashed
    Potatoes, 90
holiday party menus, 6–11
Holiday Sangria, 208
honey
    Lemon-Rosemary Chicken Wings, 45–46
    Parker House Rolls, 98–101
    Whipped Ricotta Toast with Olives &
        Almonds, 42
horseradish
    Bloody Mary Brunch Bar, 220
    Mini Crab Cakes with Spicy
        Remoulade, 65
    Special Occasion Roast Beef with
        Roasted Carrots, 83
Hot Chocolate, European-Style, with
    Peppermint Marshmallows, 204–207

I

icings. see frostings & icings
ingredients, 227
Italian Asiago Buns, 48
Italian Hoagie Party Platter, 59
Italian Wedding Soup, 97

J

Jalapeño Poppers, Prosciutto-
    Wrapped, 56

K

Kahlúa
    Chocolate Peppermint Cake, 126–128
    Dark Chocolate & Sea Salt Caramels,
        193–195
    Eggnog Tiramisu, 118
    Kahlúa Peppermint Mocha Chocolate
        Truffles, 190–192
Kirsch
    Black Forest Cheesecake, 137–138
    Cranberry Cherry Pie, 145–147

L

ladyfingers: Eggnog Tiramisu, 118
lemons
    Bloody Mary Brunch Bar, 220
    Cozy Mulled Cider, 219
    Crowd-Pleasing Caesar Salad with
        Garlic Bread Croutons, 111–112
    Herb-Crusted Salmon with Mashed
        Potatoes, 90
    Lemon Risotto with Brown Butter
        Scallops, 79–80
    Lemon-Rosemary Chicken Wings,
        45–46
    Lemon White Chocolate Macadamia
        Nut Cookies, 167
    Pan-Seared Cod in Lemon-Caper
        Sauce, 74
    Pomegranate Party Punch, 212
    Rosemary Lemonade, 215
lettuce
    Bloody Mary Brunch Bar, 220
    Italian Hoagie Party Platter, 59
limes
    Cranberry-Ginger Moscow Mules, 216
    Pomegranate Party Punch, 212

M

M&M® Cookies, Peanut Butter, 176
Macadamia Nut Cookies, Lemon White
    Chocolate, 167
Macaroni & Cheese, Creamy White
    Cheddar, 107
maple syrup
    Brown Butter-Orange Ricotta
        Pancakes, 16
    Cinnamon Apple French Toast, 35
Marinara
    in Chicken Parmesan for a Crowd,
        84–86
    in Meatball & Spinach Baked Ziti, 77
    in Ultimate Meatball Sliders, 47
Marshmallows, Peppermint, 204–207

mascarpone
    Eggnog Tiramisu, 118
    Extra Creamy Cannoli, 125
    Gingerbread Celebration Cake,
        149–150
    Mascarpone Frosting, 150
    see also cream cheese
Mashed Potatoes, Herb-Crusted Salmon
    with, 90
mayonnaise
    Four-Cheese Spinach Dip, 66
    Mini Crab Cakes with Spicy
        Remoulade, 65
meals
    Chicken Parmesan for a Crowd, 84–86
    Garlicky Shrimp Polenta, 73
    Herb-Crusted Salmon with Mashed
        Potatoes, 90
    Holiday Hens with Wild Rice Pilaf, 70
    Lemon Risotto with Brown Butter
        Scallops, 79–80
    Meatball & Spinach Baked Ziti, 77–78
    Pan-Seared Cod in Lemon-Caper
        Sauce, 74
    Rigatoni Bolognese with Garlic Bread,
        87–89
    Special Occasion Roast Beef with
        Roasted Carrots, 83
meatballs
    Italian Wedding Soup, 97
    Meatball & Spinach Baked Ziti, 77–78
    Ultimate Meatball Sliders, 47–48
menus
    choosing, 230
    holiday party, 6–11
Mimosas, Piña Colada Sunrise, 223
Mini Crab Cakes with Spicy
    Remoulade, 65
mint: Cranberry-Ginger Moscow
    Mules, 216
Mocha Chocolate Truffles, Kahlúa
    Peppermint, 190–192
molasses
    Gingerbread Celebration Cake,
        149–150
    Molasses Cream Pies, 171–172
Morning Glory Muffins, 39
Moscow Mules, Cranberry-Ginger, 216

mozzarella
    Chicken Parmesan for a Crowd, 84–86
    Four-Cheese Spinach Dip, 66
    Ultimate Meatball Sliders, 47–48
Muffins, Morning Glory, 39
Mulled Cider, Cozy, 219
music, 232
mustard, Dijon: Special Occasion Roast Beef with Roasted Carrots, 83

N

New York-Style Cheesecake with Grand Marnier® Cranberry Sauce, 121–122
Nutella® Beignets, 25–27
nutmeg: Thick & Creamy Eggnog, 211
nuts
    Brown Butter Blondies, 179
    Cherry-Almond Chocolate Bark, 182
    Chocolate-Covered Almond Toffee, 197
    Coconut-Pecan Truffles, 198
    Extra Creamy Cannoli, 125
    Feel-Good Holiday Salad, 103
    Holiday Hens with Wild Rice Pilaf, 70
    Lemon White Chocolate Macadamia Nut Cookies, 167
    Morning Glory Muffins, 39
    Nutella® Beignets, 25–27
    Warm Bacon & Green Bean Salad, 115
    Whipped Ricotta Toast with Olives & Almonds, 42

O

oats
    Oatmeal Chocolate Chunk Cookies, 160
    Salted Caramel Apple Pie Bars, 173–174
Old Bay® seasoning
    Bloody Mary Brunch Bar, 220
    Mini Crab Cakes with Spicy Remoulade, 65
olives: Whipped Ricotta Toast with Olives & Almonds, 42
onions
    Bacon & Caramelized Onion Quiche, 23–24
    Caramelized Onion Dip Snack Board, 51–52
orange marmalade: Molasses Cream Pies, 171–172
oranges
    Brie Bites with Cranberry Chutney, 60–63
    Brown Butter-Orange Ricotta Pancakes, 16
    Cozy Mulled Cider, 219
    Cranberry Orange Scones, 32
    Holiday Hens with Wild Rice Pilaf, 70
    Holiday Sangria, 208
    New York-Style Cheesecake with Grand Marnier® Cranberry Sauce, 121–122
    Orange Glaze, 32
    Piña Colada Sunrise Mimosas, 223
    Whipped Ricotta Toast with Olives & Almonds, 42
orzo: Pan-Seared Cod in Lemon-Caper Sauce, 74

P

Pancakes, Brown Butter-Orange Ricotta, 16
pancetta
    Balsamic Roasted Brussels Sprouts with Pancetta & Pomegranate Seeds, 108
    Holiday Hens with Wild Rice Pilaf, 70
    Rigatoni Bolognese with Garlic Bread, 87–89
Pan-Seared Cod in Lemon-Caper Sauce, 74
Parker House Rolls, 98–101
Parmesan
    Chicken Parmesan for a Crowd, 84–86
    Crowd-Pleasing Caesar Salad with Garlic Bread Croutons, 111–112
    Four-Cheese Spinach Dip, 66
    Garlicky Shrimp Polenta, 73
    Garlic Parmesan Popcorn, 55
    Italian Wedding Soup, 97
    Lemon Risotto with Brown Butter Scallops, 79–80
    Meatball & Spinach Baked Ziti, 77–78
    Sausage & Potato Breakfast Casserole, 28
    Ultimate Meatball Sliders, 47–48
Party Punch, Pomegranate, 212
pasta
    Chicken Parmesan for a Crowd, 84–86
    Creamy White Cheddar Macaroni & Cheese, 107
    Italian Wedding Soup, 97
    Meatball & Spinach Baked Ziti, 77–78
    Pan-Seared Cod in Lemon-Caper Sauce, 74
    Pasta Fagioli, 104
    Rigatoni Bolognese with Garlic Bread, 87–89
Peanut Butter Christmas Trees, Chocolate-Covered, 186–189
Peanut Butter M&M® Cookies, 176
pears
    Holiday Sangria, 208
    Morning Glory Muffins, 39
    Pomegranate Party Punch, 212
pecans
    Bourbon Butter Pecan Fudge, 185
    Brown Butter Blondies, 179
    Coconut-Pecan Truffles, 198
    Feel-Good Holiday Salad, 103
    Morning Glory Muffins, 39
    Pumpkin Cheesecake with Pecan Praline Sauce, 129–130
peppermint
    Chocolate Peppermint Cake, 126–128
    European-Style Hot Chocolate with Peppermint Marshmallows, 204–207
    Kahlúa Peppermint Mocha Chocolate Truffles, 190–192
    Peppermint Bark, 201
peppers, spicy
    Italian Hoagie Party Platter, 59
    Prosciutto-Wrapped Jalapeño Poppers, 56
    see also bell peppers
Pie, Cranberry Cherry, 145–147
Piña Colada Sunrise Mimosas, 223
pineapples: Piña Colada Sunrise Mimosas, 223

pistachios
    Cranberry-Pistachio Biscotti, 163–164
    Extra Creamy Cannoli, 125
    Holiday Hens with Wild Rice Pilaf, 70

planning ahead, 229–230

playlists, creating, 232

Polenta, Garlicky Shrimp, 73

pomegranates
    Balsamic Roasted Brussels Sprouts with Pancetta & Pomegranate Seeds, 108
    Feel-Good Holiday Salad, 103
    Holiday Sangria, 208
    Piña Colada Sunrise Mimosas, 223
    Pomegranate Party Punch, 212

Popcorn, Garlic Parmesan, 55

potatoes
    Herb-Crusted Salmon with Mashed Potatoes, 90
    Rosemary & Garlic Roasted Potatoes, 94
    Sausage & Potato Breakfast Casserole, 28

poultry
    Chicken Parmesan for a Crowd, 84–86
    Holiday Hens with Wild Rice Pilaf, 70
    Lemon-Rosemary Chicken Wings, 45–46

practicing, 229

Prosciutto-Wrapped Jalapeño Poppers, 56

prosecco. *see* Champagne

provolone: Italian Hoagie Party Platter, 59

Pumpkin Cheesecake with Pecan Praline Sauce, 129–130

Punch, Pomegranate Party, 212

Q

Quiche, Bacon & Caramelized Onion, 23–24

R

recipes, following, 227

Remoulade, Spicy, Mini Crab Cakes with, 65

rice
    Holiday Hens with Wild Rice Pilaf, 70
    Lemon Risotto with Brown Butter Scallops, 79–80

ricotta
    Brown Butter-Orange Ricotta Pancakes, 16
    Extra Creamy Cannoli, 125
    Meatball & Spinach Baked Ziti, 77–78
    Whipped Ricotta Toast with Olives & Almonds, 42

Rigatoni Bolognese with Garlic Bread, 87–89

Risotto, Lemon, with Brown Butter Scallops, 79–80

Roast Beef with Roasted Carrots, Special Occasion, 83

Rolls, Parker House, 98–101

rosemary
    Garlic Parmesan Popcorn, 55
    Gingerbread Celebration Cake, 149–150
    Lemon-Rosemary Chicken Wings, 45–46
    Rosemary & Garlic Roasted Potatoes, 94
    Rosemary Lemonade, 215

rum
    Chocolate-Covered Almond Toffee, 197
    Cozy Mulled Cider, 219
    Eggnog Tiramisu, 118
    Piña Colada Sunrise Mimosas, 223
    Thick & Creamy Eggnog, 211

S

salads
    Crowd-Pleasing Caesar Salad with Garlic Bread Croutons, 111–112
    Feel-Good Holiday Salad, 103

salami: Italian Hoagie Party Platter, 59

Salmon, Herb-Crusted, with Mashed Potatoes, 90

Salted Caramel Apple Pie Bars, 173–174

Salted Caramel Sauce, 174

Sandwich Cookies, in My Favorite Butter Cookies, 154–157

Sandwiches
    Italian Hoagie Party Platter, 59
    Ultimate Meatball Sliders, 47–48

Sangria, Holiday, 208

sauces & condiments
    Bolognese, 87–89
    Bourbon Maple Syrup, 16
    Brown Butter Sauce, 79
    Caesar Dressing, 111
    Cinnamon Apple Syrup, 35
    Cranberry Chutney, 63
    Grand Marnier® Cranberry Sauce, 122
    Lemon-Caper Sauce, 74
    Lemon-Rosemary Sauce, 45–46
    Marinara, 47, 77, 84–86
    Pecan Praline Sauce, 130
    Salted Caramel Sauce, 174
    Salted Honey Butter, 101
    Spicy Remoulade, 65

sausage
    Italian Wedding Soup, 97
    Meatball & Spinach Baked Ziti, 77–78
    Pasta Fagioli, 104
    Rigatoni Bolognese with Garlic Bread, 87–89
    Sausage & Potato Breakfast Casserole, 28
    Ultimate Meatball Sliders, 47–48

scales, kitchen, 227

Scallops, Brown Butter, Lemon Risotto with, 79–80

Scones, Cranberry Orange, 32

seafood
    Garlicky Shrimp Polenta, 73
    Herb-Crusted Salmon with Mashed Potatoes, 90
    Lemon Risotto with Brown Butter Scallops, 79–80
    Pan-Seared Cod in Lemon-Caper Sauce, 74
    Sea Salt Caramels, Dark Chocolate &, 193–195

Shrimp Polenta, Garlicky, 73

sides
    Balsamic Roasted Brussels Sprouts with Pancetta & Pomegranate Seeds, 108
    Creamy White Cheddar Macaroni & Cheese, 107
    Crowd-Pleasing Caesar Salad with Garlic Bread Croutons, 111–112
    Feel-Good Holiday Salad, 103

Italian Wedding Soup, 97
Parker House Rolls, 98–101
Pasta Fagioli, 104
Rosemary & Garlic Roasted Potatoes, 94
Warm Bacon & Green Bean Salad, 115
Slice & Bake Cookies, in My Favorite Butter Cookies, 154–157
Sliders, Ultimate Meatball, 47–48
soppressata: Italian Hoagie Party Platter, 59
soups
    Italian Wedding Soup, 97
    Pasta Fagioli, 104
sour cream
    Caramelized Onion Dip Snack Board, 51–52
    Four-Cheese Spinach Dip, 66
    New York-Style Cheesecake with Grand Marnier® Cranberry Sauce, 121–122
Sparkling Champagne Cupcakes, 141–142
Special Occasion Roast Beef with Roasted Carrots, 83
Spicy Remoulade, Mini Crab Cakes with, 65
spinach
    Feel-Good Holiday Salad, 103
    Four-Cheese Spinach Dip, 66
    Italian Wedding Soup, 97
    Meatball & Spinach Baked Ziti, 77–78
    Pasta Fagioli, 104
    Sausage & Potato Breakfast Casserole, 28
sprinkles: Christmas Funfetti Sheet Cake, 133–134
star anise
    Cozy Mulled Cider, 219
    Pomegranate Party Punch, 212
Sugar & Spice Donuts, 31
sweetened condensed milk
    Bourbon Butter Pecan Fudge, 185
    Dark Chocolate & Sea Salt Caramels, 193–195

T
tequila: Pomegranate Party Punch, 212
themes, 230

Thick & Creamy Eggnog, 211
Thumbprint Cookies, in My Favorite Butter Cookies, 154–157
thyme
    Caramelized Onion Dip Snack Board, 51–52
    Whipped Ricotta Toast with Olives & Almonds, 42
time, baking, 228
tips
    baking, 227–229
    entertaining, 229–232
    guest lists, 233–234
Tiramisu, Eggnog, 118
Toffee, Chocolate-Covered Almond, 197
tomatoes
    Bloody Mary Brunch Bar, 220
    Chicken Parmesan for a Crowd, 84–86
    Italian Hoagie Party Platter, 59
    Meatball & Spinach Baked Ziti, 77–78
    Pasta Fagioli, 104
    Rigatoni Bolognese with Garlic Bread, 87–89
    Ultimate Meatball Sliders, 47–48
Triple Chocolate Brownies, 159
Truffles, Coconut-Pecan, 198
Truffles, Kahlúa Peppermint Mocha Chocolate, 190–192

U
Ultimate Meatball Sliders, 47–48

V
vodka
    Bloody Mary Brunch Bar, 220
    Cranberry-Ginger Moscow Mules, 216

W
walnuts
    Morning Glory Muffins, 39
    Warm Bacon & Green Bean Salad, 115
Warm Bacon & Green Bean Salad, 115
Whipped Cream, 211
Whipped Ricotta Toast with Olives & Almonds, Whipped Ricotta Toast with Olives & Almonds, 42
white beans: Pasta Fagioli, 104
white chocolate

    Bourbon Butter Pecan Fudge, 185
    Chocolate Peppermint Cake, 126–128
    Peppermint Bark, 201
    White Chocolate Peppermint Frosting, 126
Wild Rice Pilaf, Holiday Hens with, 70
wine
    Holiday Sangria, 208
    Lemon Risotto with Brown Butter Scallops, 79–80
    Pan-Seared Cod in Lemon-Caper Sauce, 74
    Rigatoni Bolognese with Garlic Bread, 87–89

Z
Ziti, Baked, Meatball & Spinach, 77–78

Copyright © 2022 by Ashley Manila, Baker by Nature, LLC

All rights reserved. No part of this publication may be reprinted, reproduced, transmitted, or utilized in any form or by any electronic, mechanical, or other means, now known or hereafter invented, including photocopying, microfilming, and recording, or in any information retrieval system without the written permission of Ashley Manila, Baker by Nature, LLC. For inquiries regarding permissions, translations, foreign rights, audio rights, and any other forms of reproduction, please contact the publisher at BakerByNature.com/contact

Trademark Notice: Product or corporate names may be trademarks or registered trademarks, and are used only for identification and explanation without intent to infringe.

ISBN: 979-8-9853651-0-8 (Hardcover)

Printed in China

Food Photography by Joanie Simon.
Food Styling by Brendan McCaskey.

Lifestyle Photography by Rikki Snyder.

Design by Weller Smith Design, LLC.

10 9 8 7 6 5 4 3 2 1

First Edition

Published by Ashley Manila, Baker by Nature, LLC

www.bakerbynature.com